Christiane Gauthier

Jean-François Lacroix

Paul-E. Lambert

Gastronomy
and the
Forest

"O seasons, river,
alders and ferns, leaves, flowers,
wet wood, blue grasses,
all our riches bleed their fragrance,
animal musk beside us."

Anne Hébert

GOURMAND WORLD
COOKBOOK AWARDS 2003

Best Francophone Cookbook
Categories:
- Best Single Subject
- Best Innovative Cookbook
- Best Design

GOURMAND WORLD
COOKBOOK AWARDS 2003
BARCELONA

Best Cookbook in the World
In all Languages
Category: Best Single Subject

CUISINE CANADA AND
THE UNIVERSITY OF GUELPH

NATIONAL CULINARY
BOOK AWARDS 2004

Gold Award
Category: Cookbooks, French-Language

Gold Award
Category: Canadian Food Culture Book

CONCEPTION AND GRAPHIC DESIGN
Communication Publi Griffe

DIGITALIZATION
Caractéra

PRINTING
J. B. Deschamps Inc.

BINDING
Multi-Reliure

© Gesti-Faune Inc., Christiane Gauthier,
  Jean-Francois Lacroix, Paul-E. Lambert

Legal deposit, 4th trimester 2005
Bibliothèque nationale du Québec
National Library of Canada
ISBN 2-9807791-1-3
(Original edition: 2-9807791-0-5,
Éditions Gesti-Faune, Québec)

Translated by Laurent Lavigne and Anne L. Desjardins

EDITION AND DISTRIBUTION
Gesti-Faune Inc.
205, 1st Avenue
Stoneham, Québec
Canada G0A 4P0
Telephone: (418) 848-5424
Fax: (418) 848-5438
E-mail: dcraig@gestifaune.com
www.gestifaune.com

Thanks
to all those who contributed to this book through their enthusiasm and their assistance

RECIPE COLLABORATORS
Jean-Marc Couillard
Guy Ernst
Jean-Félix Giguère
Véronique Gosselin
Roxanne Harvey
Kristine Laflamme
Sonia Ratté
Patrick Rioual
Céline Turgeon

TALES COLLABORATORS
Martin Audet
Marie-France Bornais,
for the wording of the french version
Dave Boulet
David Craig
Philippe Tanguay

EDITORIAL ADVISORS AND RESEARCHERS
Esther Greaves
Nathalie Cooke
Marie-Thérèse Blanc

EDITORIAL ADVISOR
Paul Marriner

PROOFREADERS
Faye Bélanger
Jane Elias

INFORMATIC ADVISOR
Jean Lambert

COLLABORATORS FOR THE FRENCH VERSION
Fierbourg, Centre de formation professionnelle
Fonds Jeunesse Québec
Bona Beaulieu
Line Beaulieu

**LOANER OF DECORATIVE OBJECTS
FOR THE PRESENTATION OF RECIPES**
Faye Bélanger
Lynn Campbell
Diane Giguère
Raynald Girard
Serge Laroche
Jordan L. LeBel
Maryse LeBel
Pauline Laberge
Madeleine Lapierre
Lise Nicole
France St-Hilaire
Laurette Thériault
Viviane Troche

**THANKS TO THE WORKING GROUP THAT REFLECTED
ON THE PLEASURES OF BEING IN THE FOREST**
André Boucher
Michel Gauthier
Mario Lalanne
Louise Laparé
Johanne Reney

THANKS ALSO TO:
Michel Baril
Aldée Beaumont
Jacques Bérubé
Jean-Paul and Réjeanne Coudé
Fernand Dufour
Solange Doucet
Marc Girard
Benoît Magnan
Deny McDonald, *Taxidermist*
Michel Minville
Céline Morand
Michel Ste-Marie, *Lithographie du vieux Laprairie*
Louise Tougas
All Gesti-Faune employees

Foreword

Quebec is an immense territory of 1,500,000 square kilometers of diverse forests, abundant wildlife and over a million rivers and lakes, with scenery that will take your breath away. The Quebec Outfitters Federation (QOF) and their 400 members make up the largest network of lodging accommodations in Quebec forests. In both summer and winter, they offer fishing and hunting as well as numerous other outdoors activities developed to meet the needs of all people, from the most adventurous to the more reserved. Through these different outfitters, you can discover the uniqueness of each region of Quebec, the flora and the fauna that lives there, the attractions each possesses and the activities that can be enjoyed.

Quebec outfitters are managed by men and women with a passion for nature who have the well-being of their clients at heart, and who by their warm welcome and their knowledge of the territory, assure you of a memorable outdoors experience. At the forefront of sustainable development, these entrepreneurs have for decades helped to preserve the fragile equilibrium of Quebec's eco-systems through the sound management of wildlife populations and their habitat. In this way, they assure the continuity of wildlife and plant species present on their territory while at the same time allowing us to fully enjoy them.

Each region, with very different flora and fauna, offers typical dishes and several outfitters offer local products. Therefore, whether it is through the harvest of fish and game, the gathering of wild fruits and plants or the sampling of menus prepared by the chefs themselves, you will have access to quality products allowing you to prepare or simply to savour, a multitude of exquisite dishes.

The Quebec Outfitter Federation invites you to come discover gastronomy in the Quebec forest through its vast network of outfitters.

QOF
QUEBEC
OUTFITTERS
FEDERATION INC.
www.fpq.com

T his nature-related cookbook project was initiated at the Manoir Brulé Fishing Lodge in 1995 by the wildlife biologist David Craig who is also the founder, President and owner of Gesti-Faune Inc. At that time, the new chef, Jean-François Lacroix, was developing the gastronomic dining experience that has since become the pride of the Manoir Brulé. It was only several years later, January 2000, that the team of Christiane Gauthier, Paul-E. Lambert and Jean-François Lacroix was formed and started to work on the book. The recipes and photographs were for the most part realized at the various Gesti-Faune Lodges.

Gesti-Faune Inc. now operates several private high-class fishing, hunting and wildlife observation lodges in Quebec, Canada. The most prestigious of these, the "Manoir Brulé" is situated in the boreal forest just northeast of Quebec City and caters to a corporate clientele for customer entertainment, board meetings, team building and incentive programs. Craig, a passionate trout fisherman, hunter and nature lover, has been sharing that passion with Manoir Brulé guests for the last 27 years.

The trout fishing is excellent and is a direct result of their biological expertise. For example, the construction of the "Invented River", resulted in a tenfold increase (300 to 3000) in the annual harvest of speckled trout in Lake Brulé! Furthermore, the quality of this biological enhancement project was recognised by the Canadian Government in 2000, when Gesti-Faune was awarded Canada's Recreational Fisheries Award.

Gesti-Faune is now renowned internationally for their biological approach as well as for their gastronomic dining experience in the forest. Over the years, they have been awarded several Quebec Tourism Grand Prizes in recognition of outstanding services offered. The woodlands and lakes where their lodges are located have been gifted with an abundance of trout, moose, black bear as well as many other wild animal and plant species.

Whether via a company or on an individual basis, this fine book will give you a prelude of what to expect when visiting Gesti-Faune Lodges and Outfitters in Quebec, Canada.

Gesti-Faune Corporate Lodges and Outfitters

Acknowledgements

Atwood, Margaret. "You Begin." *Selected Poems II: Poems Selected and New 1976-86.* Boston: Houghton Mifflin Company, 1987. 54. Copyright 1990 by Margaret Atwood. Reprinted by permission of Oxford University Press.

Avison, Margaret. "Light." *Always Now.* Erin: The Porcupine's Quill, 2003. 381.

Bissoondath, Neil. "Pieces of Sky." *If You Love This Country - 15 Voices for a Unified Country.* Roberta L. Bondar. Toronto: Penguin Books Inc., 1992. 76.

Carman, Bliss. "Morning in the Hills." *An Anthology of Canadian Literature in English.* Eds Russell Brown, Donna Bennett, & Nathalie Cooke. Toronto: Oxford University Press, 1990. 123.

Burnford, Sheila. "*The Fields of Noon.*" Toronto: McClelland & Stewart Ltd., 1964. 16,75.

Campbell, Wilfred. "Coming Winter." *The Poetical Works of Wilfred Campbell.* London: W.J. Sykes - Hodder and Stoughton Ltd, 1922. 31.

Crozier, Lorna. "Fishing in Air." "Loon Song." *The Garden Going On Without Us.* Toronto: McClelland & Stewart Ltd., 1985. 70,72.

Drummond, William Henry. "The Voyageur." *Habitant Poems.* Toronto: McClelland & Stewart Ltd., 1926. 26.

Hébert, Anne. *Poems by Anne Hébert.* Trans. Alan Brown. Don Mills, Ontario: Musson Book Company, 1975. 49.

Howe, Joseph. "The Song of the Micmac." *100 Poems of Nineteenth-Century Canada.* Eds. Douglas Lochhead and Raymond Souster. Toronto: Macmilllan, 1974. 2.

Johnson, Pauline. "The Song My Paddle Sings." *Canadian Poets.* John W. Carvin. London: McClelland and Stewart Limited, 1926. 130.

Lalonde, Robert. *One Beautiful Day to Come.* Victoria: Originally published in English by Ekstasis Editions Canada Ltd, 1998. 35,48,52.

Lane, Patrick. *Winter.* Saskatchewan: Coteau, 1990. 2.

Layton, Irving. "The Cold Green Element." *The Collected Poems of Irving Layton.* Toronto: McClelland & Stewart Ltd., 1965.

Leclerc, Félix. *The Madman, the Kite and the Island.* Trans. Phillip Stratford. Toronto: General Publishing Co. Limited, 1983. 28.

Leacock, Stephen. *Sunshine Sketches of Stephen Leacock.* Revised and Abriged Edition. 174.

MacEwen, Gwendolyn. "Dark Pines Under Water." *The Shadow-Maker.* Toronto: Macmillan, 1972. Permission for use is granted by the author's family.

MacLeod, Alistair. "The Lost Salt Gift of Blood." *Island.* Toronto: McClelland & Stewart Ltd., 2000. 121, 122.

Marie-Victorin, Frère. *Flore Laurentienne,* Les presses de l'Université de Montréal, 1995. p.438

Miron, Gaston. "The Age of Winter." *Embers and Earth (Selected Poems).* Trans. D.G. Jones and Marc Plourde. Montréal: Guernica Editions, 1984. 25.

Montgomery, Lucy Maud. *Anne of Green Gables.* Toronto: The Ryerson Press, 1908. 242.

Ostenso, Martha. *Wild Geese.* Toronto: McClelland & Stewart Inc., 1961. 56,243.

Purdy, Al. "Trees At the Arctic Circle." *Being Alive.* Toronto: McClelland & Stewart Ltd., 1978.

Reeves, Hubert. *Oiseaux, merveilleux oiseaux, Les Dialogues du ciel et de la vie,* Éditions du Seuil/Sciences ouvertes, 1998, p.229

Roberts, Sir Charles G.D. "The Flight of the Geese." *An Anthology of Canadian Literature in English,* Revised and Abridged Edition. 115.

Rosenblatt, Joe. *The Lake.* Toronto: Exile and Exile Editions, 1985.

Roy, Gabrielle. *The Hidden Mountain.* Trans. Harry L. Binsse. Toronto: McClelland & Stewart Limited, 1962. 15,43.

Sangster, Charles. "Sonnets Written in the Orillia Woods." *Revised and Abridged Edition.* 102.

Savard, Félix-Antoine. *L'abatis,* Fides, 1943, pp.68; 92; 103

Scott, Frederick George. "Laurentian Shield." *Events and Signals.* Toronto: Ryerson Press, 1954.

Service, Robert W. *Songs of a Sourdough.* Toronto: William Briggs. 1909. 14. Produced by Canadiana – org. CIHM # 9-91677.

Sinclair, Ross. *As For Me and My House.* Toronto: McClelland & Stewart Ltd., 1957. 148.

Thoreau, Henry David. *Walden and Other Writings.* New York: Barnes & Noble Books, 1993. 165, 188.

Photo by his friend Eugène Kedl

Jean-François Lacroix

For the recipes and creation of the dishes.

Born in the shadow of the bell towers of the Basilica of Ste Anne de Beaupré, near Quebec City, Jean-François Lacroix has been immersed since his early youth in the hotel and restaurant environment. Very early on, he abandoned everyday cooking and turned to gastronomy, enrolling as a young adult at the Centre de formation professionnelle du Trait-Carré in Charlesbourg. A first culinary competition confirmed his talent: he won the bronze medal in cuisine. Stimulated by competition, Jean-François Lacroix went through all the stages of the U-S Skills Olympics in Louisville, Kentucky. His list of achievements includes an Excellence award given out by the *Société des chefs cuisiniers et pâtissiers du Québec*; and more recently, he was judged Chef of the Year for the Quebec Chapter by the same organisation.

Insatiably curious and open, the young chef specialised in pastry; he studied at the École nationale supérieure de pâtisserie in Yssingeaux, France, then at the famed École LeNôtre and École gastronomique Bellouet-conseil in Paris.

A creative bon vivant, Jean-François Lacroix honed his skills in several of the Quebec City region's best restaurants. He has been executive chef of the Gesti-Faune Corporate Outfitters for the past 9 years, and teaches cooking and pastry at the Fierbourg, centre de formation professionnelle in Charlesbourg.

Paul-E. Lambert

For the photography, creation and layout of the book.

A graduate of the New York Institute of Photography, he has been a member of many of the major professional photographers associations in Canada and the United States. Passionate about images and colours, and a seasoned traveler, Paul-E. Lambert has more than 50 years experience as a professional photographer. His career was in the forest industry, with his work illustrating numerous publications, annual reports and corporate publicity.

A lover of nature who is as comfortable under a tent in the forest as he is at home listening to music and reading, Paul-E. Lambert enjoys canoeing, hunting, fishing and an amazing array of outdoor activities. An enthusiastic fly-fisher, he just as easily teases the salmon in the rivers of Gaspesia and the Lower North Shore as he does the speckled trout in the lakes of the Laurentians and the Appalachians.

For many years, moose and caribou were his favorite targets. Now, when autumn approaches with its pungent odours of dead leaves, walking in the woods and small game attract him.

Armed with this forestry background, and almost as much a gourmand as he is a gourmet, Paul-E. Lambert hopes his images will stimulate the taste buds of fine food lovers as much as they will encourage lovers of the great outdoors to dream.

Christiane Gauthier

For the concept, research and project management as well as the testing and formulation of each recipe.

A graduate of Montreal's Hautes Études Commerciales and of the Institut de diététique et de nutrition of l'Université de Montréal, Christiane Gauthier has held various positions in food management services in both the public and private sectors. She is co-author and editor of the books "Standardization: the Key Link between Quality and Cost Ratio in Food; from Theory to Practice," "Food Cost: from Quality... to Profitability" and "The Actual Issues of Marketing in the Food and Restaurant Industries."

Christiane Gauthier is as comfortable in the urban jungle as she is in the forests of Quebec. A lover of the arts and literature, she views nature as a large book. When summer comes, she leaves the city to take advantage of the beauty of Quebec's lakes and to succumb to the pleasures of fly-fishing. Autumn brings her the challenge of deer hunting. And in winter, as an ardent fisher, she enjoys the thrill of ice fishing.

Untiring, when she is at home, all the recipes are put to test: soups, saddle of hare, stir-fries, grilled meats and soufflés, all deliver their secrets to her, and with great pleasure.

Her passion for fishing and hunting together with her love of good food brought her to this project.

Preface

Dear readers

Quebec is home to a remarkable array of fauna within the vastness of its wilderness. Only a privileged few know it well, and it is through outfitters that some of the most productive wildlife areas were discovered and made accessible. So it is completely natural that the inspiration for this book comes from an outfitter concerned about sustainability, and one who has already made his mark in the field. Here, then, is an artistic collection, in the very image of this Quebec we so love, a Quebec of mythic allure, yet nevertheless very real with its forests and its countless lakes and rivers.

We do not hesitate to call this collection art, because the images it contains are like ten-thousand-word poems that secret voices whisper to the eyes. Yes, as you leaf through this book, you will understand how it is possible to hear with your eyes. But intimately connected to the visual delights within every camera-captured landscape is a pleasure for the palate, a pleasure awaiting discovery.

Fish and game are showcased in this collection of recipes but, since wild game is not accessible to all, the authors wisely decided to share honours with dishes featuring domestic comestibles. And, as everything in this book is to be devoured, you will also delight in the colourful tales told to the editors by a few well-known guides. Finally, to enrich many of the images, are the timeless words of some great writers.

Hailed by critics, and already the winner of several prizes in its French editions, Gastronomy and the Forest is, and will remain, one of the most beautiful tributes ever paid to Quebec's natural riches.

Louise Laparé
Actress

Gaston Lepage
Actor and Host

Introduction

Can anything new be written about pleasure that hasn't been written before? After all, the pursuit of pleasure is at the heart of human behavior and has been the subject of countless articles, books, and philosophical discourses. These days, it seems, everybody is a hedonist. We desire products that excite our senses. We buy 'experiences' to improve our physical and emotional well-being. We indulgence ourselves by eating our favorite treats – all too often in secrecy or on the run. Increasingly, marketing professionals have learned to tug at our heartstrings (and loosen our purse strings!) with the promise of pleasure. Yet, in the hustle and bustle of our daily routines, we tend to forget that many pleasures are in fact simple, easily accessible, and often right under our noses. An inquisitive eye, a curious ear, a second of attention is all it takes to open the door to unexpectedly rich pleasures. Nature lovers and fishing aficionados have learned to appreciate pleasurable opportunities that many of us miss or overlook: the invigorating fresh air of a morning outing, the playful splash of the fish, the breathtaking blue and orange palette unique to a dusk sky, the fireside stories with their sometimes colorful departures from reality...

Scientists tell us that we are innately predisposed, hard-wired if you will, to seek pleasure. Still, it is up to each of us to learn and decide, usually through trial and error, what relationship we will have to pleasure and the place we will make for it in our lives. After all, beyond innate dispositions, pleasure is also a matter of exploration and personal discovery. This is why I applaud the efforts of the authors of "Gastronomy and the Forest." With refreshing charm and curiosity they have explored seemingly disparate pleasures such as food, nature, fishing, and poetry. With skillful orchestration, the authors have combined these pleasures into a happy and delectable alliance where the whole is greater than the sum of its parts.

As you begin to read this book, prepare yourself for a unique experience. This is no ordinary cookbook. It is not merely a collection of tantalizing recipes and spectacular original photography. This book is an invitation – an invitation to a meandering journey where the table becomes a gateway to explore your own pleasures. As food columnist Harriet van Horne once wrote: "Food is like love, it should be entered into with abandon or not at all." Abandon yourself to your taste buds and discover why the colors of a dusk sky can make the fish taste even more delicious.

Jordan

Jordan L. LeBel, Ph.D.
Associate Professor, Food and Beverage Management
School of Hotel Administration
Cornell University

Contents

GASTRONOMIC ESSAYS EVOKING THE PLEASURES OF BEING IN THE FOREST

On a beautiful May afternoon, just before the fishing season, seven nature lovers spoke of their diverse experiences in the forest: joy, contemplation, play, fulfilment, peace...

Each scene in this book evokes their reflections.

One little step too far

A story as told by David Craig

That day, fishing had been good on Lake Caribou. With his guests comfortably seated in the plush armchairs of Manoir Brulé after a gourmet dinner, Dave Craig regales them with amusing fishing stories, usually involving other guests and friends. In front of a fire that reflects a ruddy glow onto the Manoir's huge chimney, everyone listens...

One of our guides, François, was at Lake Vase with two Americans. They had arrived early to get the best fishing and now stood together on the tiny three-foot-wide dock.

No one had fished Vase for several days and rain water had filled the canoe, so Francois started scooping it out with a little plastic container. "Hang on a minute," one of the guests said, "that'll take forever. Let's all grab the canoe and flip it over."

"Ok," François agreed. With that, the three lined up alongside the canoe, lifted it a little, and tried to flip it onto the dock. "We can do it," someone says. Lift it higher. Back up a step. Almost got it now, but they have to back up a little bit more...

Ah, but..., that last little bit was half a bit too much, over all three went, arms flailing, tumbling backwards into the lake.

A "funniest home video" winner for certain, if only...!

Two lucky ladies

A story told by David Craig

In the early eighties the directors of a major publishing group – avid anglers all – arrived for a get-together at Manoir Brulé accompanied by their wives and several friends. Since I was the junior guide, I was assigned two of the women. Rita, one of my charges, was the wife of the Vice-President. Since neither was a gung-ho angler, they would be the last to choose their lake... not surprising as the management wanted especially to please the directors.

The next morning Adeline and Rita chose Lake Brulé from the few remaining candidates. Back then one didn't get a lot of bites in the big lake[1]. Nonetheless, the ladies learned some fly fishing techniques and succeeded in catching seven or eight trout. Back at the Manoir, to everyone's surprise, they were the only ones who had caught fish. How could this be? After all, they were neophytes fishing in the toughest lake.

On the other hand, the President and his wife had gone to the best lake, Lake Caribou, and yet come back empty-handed. The same fate, on the same lake, had befallen the Vice-President and one of his friends.

Before the next day's selections were made, I thought to myself, since nobody's taken any trout out of Lake Caribou there's a good chance it won't be picked. Instead everybody'll jump at Lake Brulé where we caught so well yesterday. So I suggested to Rita that she pick Lake Caribou because the last time I'd been there I'd found a small fishing spot full of trout. I told her, "If they're still there, the fishing will be outstanding!"

As I predicted, nobody picked Lake Caribou, and so Rita followed my recommendation. Having taught the two women the basics of fly fishing, I believed they had sufficient skill to get the job done providing the trout cooperated. It might not be pretty, but it would be effective.

As we were leaving, the ladies' husbands came by to see us off. The men got quite a razzing. So much so that, when we got into the vehicle, the women worried that they'd laid it on a little thick. "If we come back empty-handed, we're going to hear about it!"

On Lake Caribou, once we were within a hundred feet of the fishing spot, we could already see the trout jumping out of the water. I said, "Wow! They're there!" The hole wasn't very big, perhaps thirty feet square. To fish it properly I had to tie the bow to the shore and drop the anchor from the stern. Two flies adorned each leader and, well, I could say the ladies, "tossed their flies," but to be polite we'll call it fly fishing.

Each time one of the little flies touched the water, three or four trout rose for it. One or two would be landed. It was absolute madness. About an hour and a half later, we had caught our limit which, at 20 trout each, meant 40 trout. "That's it," I said, "time to stop and head back to camp."

In the main lounge of the Manoir the men were dumbfounded. They, the superior fishermen, had gone to Lake Caribou and hadn't caught anything while these two women, who supposedly didn't know much about fishing, had come back with their limit. I can tell you that at supper time the men had all they could handle!

The next day, Sunday, was the last day of the fishing season. Once again our little team headed out onto Lake Brulé. Brulé is a long, deep, dark-water lake. I knew where, in a little bay, a spring welled-up under a floating island. And there the trout would be gathering for spawning. On our arrival at the honey-hole, my sports started casting. They'd been getting better over the past two days and were now fly fishing quite respectably.

Just ahead of Rita's fly, a beautiful trout jumps. I can still see its head coming out of the water... pow! The trout "strikes" the fly. Rita sees the trout and hooks it. Now she has a real big one at the end of her line! Self-control evaporates. She's reeling in the line – I'm telling her what to do, shouting, but she can't hear me at all – total panic! Finally, I scoop the trout with the net just before it passes through the guides of the fishing rod!

It turned out to be the largest trout of the year and Rita's exploit has been immortalized with a souvenir plaque at the Manoir. It was also then that the little bay was named Dave's Bay. Contrary to what many people believe, it's not because of the Invented River, but rather to commemorate this extraordinary day!

[1] Today Lake Brulé has become the best lake at the Lodge because of the construction of the "Invented River" and its spawning beds.

Observations from a hunt at Manoir Brulé

Story told by Martin Audet (and written by C. Gauthier)

This is a story about a fall hunt, a moose hunt, a bow and arrow hunt. What makes it unusual is that the hunter brought along his wife as an observer. The winds are light and dry when our hunter Laurier arrives; the calls will carry very well. We talk a little about strategy and of the signs we've seen. Now it's three o'clock in the afternoon. We're excited and so decide to take a walk up to the top of Lake Chien. Up there is a tranquil marsh, crossed by a little stream surrounded by moss, with fir trees on either side. It's a great place to observe an animal in the open.

We walk quietly up the trail heading for the top of Lake Chien. On the way we stop and slosh around in several small bays to imitate a moose. We utter a few soft female calls too. With the stops it takes a good hour to get there and then we need a few more

minutes to catch our breath. No wind stirs the trees so the calls will carry well, and with only a few birds singing and squirrels chattering, if anything approaches we'll hear it.

I put Laurier's wife on a big rock so she can see everything, including us. I tell her, "If a moose comes toward us, don't move!"

I position myself so that if a moose shows up, I can call it toward me, and the hunter will have a good line of fire. Laurier imitates a female call, it carries well. Next we hear a slight cracking, but it could be just the squirrels. We look at each other questioningly, but unsure we wait. He gives another call. Five minutes later, CRACK. Just once, CRACK. It's certainly not a squirrel! Must be a large branch breaking. The two of us stare at each other again; we hear nothing more, nothing at all.

Now I looked up at Laurier's wife; she was signaling me with her eyes that there were moose. I was looking at her and trying to make her signs: one, or two? She was making me signs: no, no, no. Is it a bear? No! Finally I understood; three moose! She could see all of this quite clearly. From ground level, Laurier and I couldn't see through the fir trees; but we could easily feel the moss trembling underfoot. Everything was shaking because there were three animals, including a female that must easily have been 800 pounds. The two males were smaller, still it was three huge beasts that were moving, walking, sometimes even running on the other side of the stream. We began making bull calls and breaking branches. Almost every time we called the larger male came toward the stream, toward us, but without crossing. Several times he walked into the stream, raking his antlers through the water to warn "us" off. However, whenever the big bull showed interest in us, the little male headed for the female, so the big fellow would forget about us to go chase him off.

The show included locking horns. And, the hunter's wife could see it all. Whereas us...

...Crouched on the ground, knees in the water, soaking wet, what to do? My hunter kept making me broad signs for: "I can't see them, I can't see them". Should he move? Should we wait? What next? The moose were on the other side of the stream for a good fifteen minutes. We were bugging them by playing the third male, but they didn't want to come across, and we were beginning to worry that they'd lose interest and leave. We agreed that Laurier would try to climb up toward the creek so that he could at least see them, and perhaps get in range for a shot. Just at that moment the female spotted me, she backed off and then took off running. But not far, and when she turned back and didn't see anything, she calmed down. That's when Laurier started climbing up the hill, through the fir trees. Then all three animals headed for the woods. Laurier instinctively let loose a short bull call that stopped the males. They turned around and took two or three steps toward us – the rut is so strong! Sadly, they were still out of range for a shot and finally moved off into the woods.

Our hunt was unsuccessful, but that moose calling experience would become an oft-told story at the Manoir.

That night, after we had returned to the Manoir, one of the guides thought he heard wolves. So he tried his hand at wolf calls. They answered back from both sides of the lodge – very powerful howls, cries that made the hair on the back of our necks bristle.

Laurier's wife relived that day for the next 3 nights. Thrilled by her experience, she was seeing moose and wolves in all her dreams.

"Under the limp leaf and the bowed branch, whilst in my hand rolls,
like berries, a water round and black, I look."

Félix-Antoine Savard

Bisque of Crayfish
from our Rivers

Serves 4

FISH STOCK

	bones, heads and trimmings of fish
30 ml (2 Tbsp)	butter
1	carrot
1	onion
1 stalk	celery
1	bay leaf
1	small carrot
1	small onion
1	shallot
1 sprig	parsley
40 g (3 Tbsp)	butter
18	river crayfish (deveined)[1]
45 ml (3 Tbsp)	Cognac
1 pinch	thyme
1	bay leaf
100 ml ($^1/_3$ cup)	dry white wine
1.5 L ($6^1/_2$ cups)	fish stock, *or* chicken stock
75 g ($^1/_2$ cup)	uncooked rice
150 ml ($^2/_3$ cup)	whipping cream
1 pinch	Cayenne pepper
30 ml (2 Tbsp)	tomato paste

PREPARATION OF THE FISH STOCK

Sweat fish bones and vegetables in butter.
Cover with cold water, bring to a boil, skim, reduce heat and infuse, covered, for 20 minutes. Strain fish stock.

PREPARATION

Dice carrot, onion and shallot. Cut parsley.

PROCEDURE

In a saucepan, melt butter over medium heat. Add diced vegetables and parsley. Sauté, without colouring, for 2 minutes.
Rinse crayfish. Add to vegetables and sauté over high heat to colour. When crayfish are red, add Cognac and flambé. Add thyme, bay leaf, white wine, a little salt and pepper. Cover and simmer 10 minutes.
In a stockpot, pour fish or chicken stock. Add rice, bring to a boil and simmer, covered, for about 20 minutes.
Remove cooked crayfish from the pot, shell, save meat from the tails, and cut into small pieces, set aside. Crush shells in a food processor or with a knife.
Pour stock and rice in a blender and process until smooth. Add crushed crayfish shells to stock. Simmer 5 minutes. Strain the bisque through a sieve.

FINAL PREPARATION

Bring bisque to a boil. Add whipping cream, Cayenne pepper and crayfish pieces. Adjust seasoning and correct colour and flavour with tomato paste. Serve hot in warm soup bowls.

[1] **Deveining:** *Remove crayfish intestine by pulling the central, round part of the tail in a circular motion.*

Crayfish is little known in Quebec.
Is that because it hides in the shelters
of the cold crystalline waters of our rivers?
It's fine and subtly flavoured
meat is a marvel to discover.

"My forest cabin half-way up the glen
Is solitary, save for one wise thrush,

The sound of falling water, and the wind
Mysteriously conversing with the leaves."

Bliss Carman

Oven Pork and Beans

1 L (4 cups)	white beans
340 g (³/₄ lb)	lean salt pork
1	onion
125 ml (¹/₂ cup)	maple syrup
125 ml (¹/₂ cup)	tomato ketchup
15 ml (1 Tbsp)	dry mustard

PREPARATION, THE DAY BEFORE
Soak beans in a large quantity of cold water and place in the refrigerator overnight.

PROCEDURE
Drain beans, place in a large pot and cover with cold water. Bring to a boil and simmer for about an hour. Drain.
Cut salt pork into thick slices. Place about half the beans in a clay pot, add half the salt pork, place the onion in the center and cover with remaining beans. Top with the rest of the salt pork. Mix together maple syrup, ketchup and dry mustard. Pour over beans and add pepper. Fill the clay pot to the rim with cold water. Cover and cook in the oven at 135°C (275°F) for 5 to 6 hours.
After a few hours, check the level of the liquid, adding water if needed. Season to taste.

FINAL PREPARATION
Remove cover for the last half hour of cooking.

Green Peppercorn Tongue Rillettes

2	veal *or* venison tongues
1.5 kg (3 lb)	pork shoulder
2	onions, studded with four whole cloves
2	bay leaves
5 ml (1 tsp)	thyme
15 ml (1 Tbsp)	chopped parsley
5 ml (1 tsp)	garlic powder, *or* 2 cloves of garlic
15 ml (1 Tbsp)	green peppercorns in brine

PROCEDURE, 24 HOURS IN ADVANCE
Cover tongues and pork with water, add cloved onions, herbs and garlic.
Cook, covered, until pork falls from the bone and skin can easily be removed from the tongues.
Cool. Remove skin and take the meat off the bone. Reserve cooking juices.
Crush green peppercorns and rake the meat into small shreds. Mix well and adjust seasoning. Place into terrine moulds.
Reduce cooking juices by about two-thirds. The texture should be syrupy. Adjust seasoning. Pour cooking juices onto the terrines so that rillettes are covered evenly.
Refrigerate.

Recipe by Jean-Marc Couillard

Game Sausage

Makes 1.5 kg (3 lb)

	sheep gut skin
3 slices	stale bread with crust removed
250 ml (1 cup)	milk
700 g (1¹/₂ lb)	ground fatty pork shoulder
750 g (1²/₃ lb)	ground game meat
1	medium onion, finely chopped
5 ml (1 tsp)	garlic powder *or* 1 clove garlic crushed
5 ml (1 tsp)	cinnamon
5 ml (1 tsp)	ginger
1	egg
60 ml (¹/₄ cup)	dry white wine

ONION CONFIT

250 ml (1 cup)	water
250 ml (1 cup)	granulated sugar
4	onions, thinly sliced

PROCEDURE, 24 HOURS IN ADVANCE
Cover sheep gut skins in water to soften for easier handling.
Saturate bread with milk, then squeeze out excess milk.
Mix together all ingredients, except white wine. Season with salt and pepper.
Pass ingredients through a meat grinder, using small cutting plate.
Cover and rest in refrigerator overnight. To test the texture and seasoning, take a small sample and cook in a frying pan. Add white wine as needed.
Using a meat grinder and sausage-stuffing funnel, stuff the sausage meat into the sheep gut. Tie off with knot at desired length.

PREPARATION OF ONION CONFIT
Bring water and sugar mixture to a boil. Add thinly sliced onions. Reduce to desired consistency.

FINAL PREPARATION AND PRESENTATION
Fry sausages in oil or butter, browning well, and serve with onion or a carrot confit.

Recipe by Jean-Marc Couillard

Trout Gravlax
with Vodka Bitter Cream

Serves 4

400 g (1 lb)	trout fillets
45 ml (3 Tbsp)	unrefined coarse salt
20 ml (4 tsp)	granulated sugar
20 ml (4 tsp)	white pepper
1 sprig	dill

VODKA BITTER CREAM

60 ml (¼ cup)	whipping cream
7 ml (1½ tsp)	lemon juice
20 ml (4 tsp)	vodka

PROCEDURE, 48 HOURS IN ADVANCE

With a small pair of tweezers, remove fish bones from trout fillets.

Place half of the fillets on a plate, skin side down.

Mix together coarse salt, sugar and white pepper.

Garnish fillets with roughly chopped dill and sprinkle with salt mixture. Cover with remaining fillets, with skin side up.

Cover with plastic wrap. Place a plate over fillets, and add a weight (a can) to apply pressure on gravlax. Refrigerate 48 hours. Turn fillets 2 or 3 times a day.

After 48 hours, remove dill and spices and wipe fillets. Check seasoning. Set aside in refrigerator.

PREPARATION OF VODKA BITTER CREAM

In a bowl, pour the cream and whip gently until it thickens, but does not form peaks. Add lemon juice and vodka and mix. Adjust seasoning.

FINAL PREPARATION AND PRESENTATION

Cut trout fillets diagonally in very thin slices. Place on a cold plate. Serve with vodka bitter cream, garnish with dill and sprinkle with coarse salt.

"The sky very deep, very blue,
very clean, not a wrinkle.
And what gold in the air!"

Félix Leclerc

"The churr of the frogs had begun in the ditches along the road,
    and the small leaves on the willows hung with a faint indolence."

Martha Ostenso

Braised Young Rabbit and Veal Sweetbreads Crépinettes
Clover Honey Sauce

Serves 4

340 g (³/₄ lb)	veal sweetbreads
30 ml (2 Tbsp)	vegetable oil
1	carrot, sliced
1	onion, thinly sliced
1 stalk	celery, thinly sliced
1	leek, thinly sliced
1 sprig	thyme
2 cloves	garlic, chopped
60 ml (4 Tbsp)	clover honey
250 ml (1 cup)	dry white wine
500 ml (2 cups)	brown veal stock
225 g (¹/₂ lb)	pig's caul
60 ml (4 Tbsp)	parsley, chopped
1	young rabbit, deboned
45 ml (3 Tbsp)	vegetable oil

BROWN STOCK OF VEAL, CHICKEN, LAMB OR VENISON AND DEMI-GLACE

Makes 2 L (8 cups) of stock

2 kg (4.4 lb)	veal, lamb, chicken *or* venison bones
1	large onion
4	carrots
3 stalks	celery
¹/₂ bulb	garlic, unpeeled
6	mushrooms
60 ml (4 Tbsp)	tomato paste
1	leek
1	bouquet garni (thyme, peppercorns, bay leaf)
	cold water

PREPARATION, 24 HOURS IN ADVANCE

Soak the veal sweetbreads in cold water and place overnight in refrigerator.

Place sweetbreads in a saucepan, and cover with cold water. Bring to a boil. Simmer for 2 minutes. Remove from heat and drain sweetbreads. Cool.

Remove membrane from sweetbreads. Place sweetbreads between two plates with a weight on top. Cool in refrigerator for several hours.

PREPARATION OF BROWN STOCK, 10 HOURS IN ADVANCE

Preheat oven to 200°C (400°F). In a roasting pan, place the bones and roast until well browned, turning occasionally. Add chopped onion, carrots, celery, garlic, mushrooms and tomato paste, mixing after 20 minutes. Continue to roast for 20 minutes or until tomato paste darkens. Add leek and continue cooking for a few minutes. Pour into a large stockpot, cover with cold water and bring to a boil. Skim, and add the bouquet garni. Simmer at low heat for 6 to 7 hours. Add water if stock reduces too much. Pass stock through a chinois or a sieve. Cool and skim off fat. Keep in freezer.

TO MAKE A DEMI-GLACE

Reduce stock by half.

PREPARATION OF CLOVER HONEY SAUCE

In a large cooking pot, heat oil, add carrot, onion, celery, leek, thyme and cloves of garlic. Sweat for 10 minutes. Add clover honey and caramelize for 2 to 3 minutes. Add white wine and reduce by half. Add brown stock and sweetbreads and bring to a boil. Cover and simmer for 20 minutes. Remove sweetbreads and cool. Reserve stock to cook crépinettes.

PROCEDURE

Spread out pig's caul and sprinkle with chopped parsley, then cut into four pieces.

Cut young rabbit in two, lengthwise from head to tail, and cut each half in two. Place on caul and season with salt and pepper. Cut sweetbreads in four and place on each piece. Wrap caul tightly around the meat to form crépinettes.

In a frying pan, heat oil and brown crépinettes on all sides. Place in the cooking pot containing the honey sauce. Bring to a boil, cover and simmer for 15 minutes. Remove from heat.

FINAL PREPARATION AND PRESENTATION

Cut crépinettes into slices, place on warm plates and serve with sauce.

Trout Rillettes

Serves 6

HOMEMADE MAYONNAISE (OPTIONAL)

2	egg yolks
5 ml (1 tsp)	Dijon mustard
2.5 ml ($^1/_2$ tsp)	salt
1 pinch	white pepper
125 ml ($^1/_2$ cup)	olive oil
30 ml (2 Tbsp)	lemon juice

REMOULADE SAUCE

125 ml ($^1/_2$ cup)	mayonnaise
15 ml (1 Tbsp)	finely chopped gherkins
15 ml (1 Tbsp)	chopped herbs (parsley, chive, chervil, tarragon)
15 ml (1 Tbsp)	capers, finely chopped
A few drops	anchovy extract
225 g ($^1/_2$ lb)	trout fillets
50 g (3 Tbsp)	unsalted butter
1 pinch	salt
1 pinch	pepper
50 ml (3 Tbsp)	mayonnaise
50 ml (3 Tbsp)	whipping cream

PREPARATION OF MAYONNAISE

In a bowl, whisk egg yolks and mustard. Add salt, pepper and mix well. Beating constantly, slowly add oil in a thin but steady stream, until mayonnaise thickens. Warm lemon juice and whisk it in the mayonnaise.

PROCEDURE, 24 HOURS IN ADVANCE

Steam the deboned trout fillets or cook in microwave oven (cook for 1 minute, stop, repeat until trout is cooked but still pink). Cool.

Beat butter until creamy. Add cold trout meat, salt, pepper, mayonnaise and cream. Mix well.

Line a bread mould or another type of mould with plastic wrap. Spread rillettes mixture into the mould. Carefully flatten the top. Cover and refrigerate 24 hours.

PREPARATION OF REMOULADE SAUCE

Mix mayonnaise with all other ingredients of remoulade sauce.

PRESENTATION

Slice rillettes and place on a chilled plate. Serve with remoulade sauce.

Lamb Chops
Fresh Rosemary Juices with Sweet Garlic Flans

Serves 4

1 kg (2 lb)	lamb chops
45 ml (3 Tbsp)	olive oil
To garnish	fresh rosemary sprigs

MARINADE

50 ml (¹/₄ cup)	red wine vinegar
100 ml (¹/₃ cup)	olive oil
1	chopped shallot
2	rosemary sprigs
1 clove	chopped garlic

SWEET GARLIC FLANS

1 bulb	garlic
15 ml (1 Tbsp)	olive oil
15 ml (1 Tbsp)	water
3	eggs
250 ml (1 cup)	whipping cream

SAUCE

125 ml (¹/₂ cup)	dry red wine
1	chopped shallot
1	pinch fresh rosemary
500 ml (2 cups)	lamb stock¹

PREPARATION OF MARINADE, A FEW HOURS IN ADVANCE

Mix red wine vinegar, olive oil, shallot, chopped rosemary, garlic and pepper. Pour over lamb chops, cover and set aside a few hours in refrigerator.

PREPARATION OF SWEET GARLIC FLANS

Preheat the oven to 160°C (325°F).

Slice garlic bulb in two, brush with olive oil. Place on a baking sheet, add a pinch of salt and water. Cover tightly with aluminum foil and bake 45 minutes to an hour, or until garlic is tender. Cool.

Press garlic bulb to remove cloves from skin. In a blender, purée garlic, add eggs and cream. Season to taste. Pour into four lightly buttered ramekins. Place ramekins in a baking pan half-filled with boiling water. Bake for 50 minutes or until flans are firm.

PREPARATION OF THE SAUCE

In a small saucepan, pour red wine, add chopped shallot and rosemary and reduce almost completely. Add lamb stock, reduce by half to concentrate flavours. Season to taste and keep warm.

PROCEDURE

Drain and pat dry lamb chops.

Place a frying pan on high heat and add olive oil. Sear lamb chops 1 or 2 minutes each side, depending on thickness. Keep warm.

PRESENTATION

In a warm plate, place lamb chops and cover with sauce. Carefully remove each garlic flan from ramekin and put on plate. Garnish with a sprig of fresh rosemary.

¹ *Lamb stock is prepared as is veal stock, substituting lamb bones for those of veal (see recipe).*

"Their seed pods glow
like delicate grey earrings
their leaves are veined and intricate
like tiny parkas
They have about three months

to make sure the species does not die
and that's how they spend their time
unbothered by any human opinion
just digging in here and now
sending their roots down down down..."

Al Purdy

Smoked Trout

Small trout
Coarse salt
Lemon juice

Maple wood saw dust
Fire wood (maple *or* birch)

SALTING
Clean trout without removing heads. Pat dry. In a thightly sealed container, place trout on their back on a thin bed of coarse salt. Add 5 or 6 drops lemon juice in each trout cavity and a pinch of coarse salt.
Cover tightly and refrigerate 10 to 12 hours.

PREPARATION FOR SMOKING
Prepare a bed of hot coals.
Lay a bed of 25 cm (10 in) saw dust, leaving only a 2 to 3 cm (1 in) opening to start the smoking process.

PREPARATION OF TROUT
Wash trout to remove excess salt. Pat dry.
In the smoker, hang trout by the head, as high as possible.

SMOKING
Smoke for about 5 hours.
Maintain heat intensity by burning 4 or 5 pieces of wood, about 5 cm by 20 cm (2 in by 8 in).
Place another bed of saw dust and smoke again. Occasionally, check trout doneness. Total cooking time varies between 6 to 12 hours, depending on climatic conditions. Avoid overcooking, so trout remain whole.
If needed, complete the cooking process in the oven. Refrigerate.

Recipe as told by Martin Audet

"The silver-turning fish is drawn toward the rock. In the shallows he flips and arcs, his flashing body breaking the water's surface as he walks upon his tail. The small fisherman has now his rod almost completely vertical. Its tip sings and vibrates high above his head while at his feet the trout spins and curves... He does not know whether he should relinquish the rod and grasp at the lurching trout or merely heave the rod backward and flip the fish behind him."

Alistair MacLeod

First Nations Bannock Bread
with Fresh and Smoked Trout

Serves 8

100 g (4 oz)	trout fillets
30 ml (2 Tbsp)	olive oil
Juice of	1 lemon
300 g (1¹/₂ cups)	flour
75 g (¹/₂ cup)	cornmeal
7.5 ml (1¹/₂ tsp)	salt
30 ml (2 Tbsp)	baking powder
300 ml (1¹/₄ cups)	water
30 ml (2 Tbsp)	capers
1 small	red onion, thinly sliced
15 ml (1 Tbsp)	hemp seeds (optional)
50 ml (3 Tbsp)	olive oil *or* hemp oil
50 g (2 oz)	smoked trout

PREPARATION OF TROUT
Cut the fresh trout fillets in strips. In a bowl, mix trout strips, olive oil, lemon juice, salt and pepper. Marinate for 20 minutes.

PREPARATION OF BANNOCK BREAD
Preheat oven to 200°C (400°F).
In a bowl, mix flour, cornmeal, salt and baking powder. Add water and stir with a fork. Do not stir too much, so as not to make the dough too elastic.
Place the dough on an oiled baking sheet. Sprinkle with a bit of flour and spread dough in order to form a circle of about 30 cm (12 in). Place fresh marinated trout, capers, onion rings and hemp seeds on the dough. Brush with oil.
Bake for 30 to 35 minutes, until bannock is golden brown.
A few minutes before baking is complete, add smoked trout, cut into strips.
Remove from the oven, and brush again with oil.

PRESENTATION
Cut bannock bread into wedges and serve warm.

Inuksuk

"Who can follow the Moose, or the wild Cariboo,
      with a footstep as light and unwearied as he?
Who can bring down the Loon with an arrow so true,
      or paddle his bark o'er stormy a sea?"

Joseph Howe

Trout en Colère

Serves 4

PIKE MOUSSE

150 g (1/3 lb)	pike fillets
175 ml (2/3 cup)	whipping cream
2.5 ml (1/2 tsp)	salt
1 pinch	pepper
1/2 pkg	fresh spinach
4	trout
250 ml (1 cup)	fish stock

SAUCE

30 ml (2 Tbsp)	chopped shallot
1 large	chopped green pepper
80 ml (1/3 cup)	dry white wine
250 ml (1 cup)	fish stock
80 ml (1/3 cup)	whipping cream

FISH STOCK

30 g (2 Tbsp)	butter
1	carrot
1	onion
2 stalks	celery
1	bay leaf
1 kg (2 lb)	fish bones, with heads and trimmings

PREPARATION OF THE PIKE MOUSSE

In a food processor, purée the pike fillets. While blending, add cream. Add salt and pepper. Pass through a sieve. Cover and refrigerate.

Wash spinach and remove stems; place in a bowl. Pour large amount of boiling water on spinach. Drain and wring spinach immediately. Set aside.

PREPARATION OF THE TROUT

Cut the trout along the belly. Debone carefully and remove the spine. Season the inside with salt and pepper, place spinach leaves inside the trout, and stuff with pike mousse. Fold the trout onto itself; pull its tail through its mouth. Set aside in refrigerator.

PREPARATION OF FISH STOCK

Sweat vegetables in butter a few minutes. Add bay leaf, fish bones and trimmings and cover with water. Bring to a boil, cover and remove from heat, infuse for 20 minutes. Strain the fish stock through a chinois or a fine sieve. Refrigerate.

PREPARATION OF THE SAUCE

In a saucepan, bring white wine shallot and green pepper to a boil. Reduce by half. Add fish stock and simmer for 5 minutes. In a blender, purée the sauce, then pour back into saucepan through a sieve and add whipping cream. Simmer for 5 more minutes, season and set aside, keeping warm.

PROCEDURE

Preheat oven to 180°C (350°F).
Place trout on a buttered pan or Dutch-oven, add hot fish stock and cover. Place in oven for 5 minutes, or until cooked. The fish stock can be kept for future use.

PRESENTATION

Place the trout on warm plates. Serve with the sauce.

"Another line zings tautly through the water,
    throwing off fine showers of iridescent droplets.
The shouts and contagious excitement spread anew..."

Alistair MacLeod

"The anticipation of the story-telling, that suffocating joy with which Jacob, this evening on the wharf, will relate the enchantment of silver and gold... time has suddenly stopped, intense, like biting heat in the chest, like paralysis. The eternal side and the fugitive side of this extraordinary moment..."

Robert Lalonde

Hazelnut Trout Fillets
Saffron Sauce

Serves 2

3	trout
70 g (¹/2 cup)	crushed hazelnuts
30 ml (2 Tbsp)	olive oil

SAFFRON SAUCE

1	chopped shallot
15 ml (1 Tbsp)	olive oil
60 ml (¹/4 cup)	dry white wine
1 ml (¹/4 tsp)	white pepper
125 ml (¹/2 cup)	fish stock
1 pinch	saffron
60 ml (¹/4 cup)	whipping cream
30 ml (2 Tbsp)	butter

PREPARATION OF TROUT
Fillet the trout, pat dry and cover with crushed hazelnuts.

PREPARATION OF SAUCE
Sweat shallot in olive oil. Add white wine, pepper, fish stock and saffron. Reduce by half. Add cream. Thicken by adding butter in small quantities, stirring constantly. Season.

PROCEDURE
Pan fry the trout fillets in oil.

PRESENTATION
In a warm plate, crisscross fillets. Serve with the hot sauce.

Recipe by Roxanne Harvey

Smoked Scallops
on a Bed of Salad

Serves 4

340 g (³/4 lb)	large fresh scallops
5 ml (1 tsp)	sea salt
5 ml (1 tsp)	granulated sugar
60 ml (¹/4 cup)	maple *or* other hardwood shavings

DRESSING
15 ml (1 Tbsp)	honey
45 ml (3 Tbsp)	white wine vinegar
125 ml (¹/2 cup)	olive oil
5 ml (1 tsp)	finely chopped shallot
2.5 ml (¹/2 tsp)	lime juice
2.5 ml (¹/2 tsp)	chopped fresh dill
5 ml (1 tsp)	salt
	pepper

SALAD
2	endives
1 L (4 cups)	mesclun

PREPARATION, A FEW HOURS IN ADVANCE
Remove the side muscle from the scallops. Place scallops in a glass bowl and sprinkle with salt and sugar. Cover and refrigerate 2 to 3 hours.

PREPARATION OF DRESSING
In a small bowl, mix honey, wine vinegar and olive oil with a whisk. Add chopped shallot, lime juice, chopped dill, salt and pepper. Stir well and set aside.

PROCEDURE
Prepare the smoker according to manufacturer's instructions, or use an old pot fitted with a grill and a lid. Heat and add hardwood shavings.
Carefully pat dry scallops, place on the grill and smoke, covered, for 10 minutes. Cool and repeat the smoking for another 10 minutes. Make sure heat is not too intense to avoid cooking the scallops. Remove them from the smoker and refrigerate.
Wash and dry mesclun and shred gently. Break off leaves from the endives, keeping 12 whole and chopping up the remainder.

FINAL PREPARATION AND PRESENTATION
Mix salad and chopped endives. Add dressing and toss. Place endive leaves on plates. Top with salad. Cut scallops into thin slices, and arrange on the salad.

"There is something he has never caught,
something that makes him stand here
every evening, casting, casting
and reeling in.

Every time he fishes he is different.
The water is different, the sky, the way
the tern hangs in the air or doesn't."

Lorna Crozier

Wintergreen tea

This plant is found in peat-bogs, humid wooded terrain and on mountain flanks. Fresh leaves are tied into small bundles with thin bands of hardwood and infused in hot water.

Labrador Tea

The infusion of the leaves has often been used as tea by people living in the forest. Apparently, it is a mild narcotic. First Nations women from different tribes drink it three times a day when delivery day approaches, and powdered leaves are used to cure headaches.

Frère Marie-Victorin

"Plunging into this fresh, new landscape, he felt deep within him that nothing of what he might discover would ever be lost to him in his memory."

Trout Soup
and Rouille

Serves 4

ROUILLE

3 cloves	garlic
1 pinch	coarse salt
2 pinches	ground pepper
1 pinch	saffron
2 pinches	Cayenne pepper
2	egg yolks
250 ml (1 cup)	olive oil
15 ml (1 Tbsp)	boiling water
1	onion
1 stalk	celery
2	carrots
2	tomatoes
15 ml (1 Tbsp)	olive oil
125 ml ($^1/_2$ cup)	dry white wine
5 pistils	saffron
1 L (4 cups)	fish stock
100 g (4 oz)	trout fillets

GARNISH

125 ml ($^1/_2$ cup)	grated Gruyère cheese
8	toasted baguette

PREPARATION OF THE ROUILLE
Chop garlic finely, mix with coarse salt, pepper, saffron, Cayenne pepper and egg yolks. Whisk well.
Add olive oil in a fine, steady stream, whisking vigorously, as you would for mayonnaise. At the end, add boiling water and whisk well.

PROCEDURE
Slice onion, julienne-cut celery and carrots. Skin, remove seeds and dice tomatoes.
In a Dutch-oven, heat the olive oil. Sweat onion, celery and carrots. When the vegetables are tender, add tomatoes, white wine and saffron. Cook 2 minutes. Add fish stock and continue cooking for 10 minutes. Add trout fillets cut into strips and cook about 4 minutes. Season with salt and pepper.

PRESENTATION
Serve trout soup in warm bowls, with rouille, toasted baguette slices and grated Gruyère cheese.

Manoir Brulé Trout Pie

1	unbaked pie pastry
15 ml (1 Tbsp)	flour
15 ml (1 Tbsp)	butter
250 ml (1 cup)	milk
1 pinch	nutmeg
450 g (1 lb)	trout fillets
100 g (1/2 cup)	onions
100 g (1 cup)	mushrooms
30 ml (2 Tbsp)	butter
150 g (5 oz)	mixture of grated Cheddar, Swiss and Mozzarella cheeses

PREPARATION
Preheat oven to 200°C (400°F).
Line a 23 cm (9 in) pie plate with pastry. Cook for 10 minutes until half-baked. Set aside. Lower oven temperature to 180°C (350°F).

PREPARATION OF BÉCHAMEL
In a saucepan, melt butter, add flour, and whisk well to obtain a white roux. Whisking constantly, add milk and nutmeg, until mixture boils. Reduce heat, simmer and season with salt and pepper.

PROCEDURE
Finely slice onions and mushrooms.
In a frying pan, sweat onions and mushrooms in butter. Set aside.
Cook trout fillets until almost done. Cool.
Place trout, onions and mushrooms in pie crust. Season with salt and pepper. Pour in Béchamel and cover with cheese mixture. Return pie to oven and bake on the lowest rack for 25 minutes or until crust is golden.

PRESENTATION
Cut the pie in pieces and serve from the cooking plate.

"...loath to come in until the last possible moment,
    and watch a spectacular sunset flaming in wild, windblown, ragged clouds:
        the air below is still and soft and full of evening sounds..."

Snail Profiteroles
in Parsley Cream

Serves 6

CHOUX PASTRY

120 g (1/2 cup)	small shrimps
250 ml (1 cup)	water
5 ml (1 tsp)	salt
100 g (1/4 cup + 2 Tbsp)	butter
165 g (1 cup + 2 Tbsp)	flour
6	eggs, medium

PARSLEY CREAM

45 ml (3 Tbsp)	chopped shallot
50 ml (1/4 cup)	dry white wine
1 bunch	fresh parsley
250 ml (1 cup)	whipping cream
80 ml (1/3 cup)	fish stock
50 g (3 Tbsp)	garlic butter
24	snails
1	tomato, diced
4 sprigs	fresh parsley

PREPARATION OF SHRIMP POWDER, A FEW HOURS IN ADVANCE

Place the shrimps on a cooking sheet in the oven for a few hours at 90°C (200°F), until completely dry. In a food processor, reduce to a powder. In this recipe, shrimp powder adds a delicate flavour to the choux pastry.

PREPARATION OF CHOUX PASTRY

In a saucepan, add water, butter and salt. Bring to a boil. Remove from heat and add all the flour at once, stirring well. Return to heat and cook for a few minutes, beating until mixture pulls away from the sides of the saucepan, forming a ball of dough.

Place choux pastry in a bowl and cool for a few minutes. Preheat oven to 200°C (400°F).

Add 5 eggs, one at a time, to the pastry, beating with each addition. Add 30 ml (2 Tbsp) shrimp powder. The pastry should be slightly runny in order to be able to use a pastry bag with a medium plain tip. Make small profiteroles, about the size of a large olive. Brush the profiteroles with a mixture of 1 egg beaten with water and salt, to brown. Bake for about 10 minutes, or until profiteroles are golden.

PREPARATION OF THE PARSLEY CREAM

In a saucepan, pour white wine, add chopped shallot and reduce by half.

Remove stems from parsley and add it to the white wine reduction. Add cream and fish stock. Boil for several minutes, until sauce coats the back of a spoon. Mix in a blender, and pass through a fine sieve. Season to taste.

PROCEDURE

In a frying pan, melt garlic butter, add snails and heat through.

FINAL PREPARATION AND PRESENTATION

Cut tops off profiteroles so to open them. Place a snail in each profiterole and replace the top. Cover a plate with the parsley cream. Place 5 profiteroles on the plate. Garnish with diced tomatoes and a sprig of parsley.

Marinated Trout Fillets Cooked on Stone
with Various Sauces

Serves 4

450 g (1 lb)	trout fillets
1	lemon
45 ml (3 Tbsp)	olive oil
1 sprig	thyme

DIJONNAISE SAUCE
125 ml (¹/₂ cup)	mayonnaise
15 ml (1 Tbsp)	Dijon mustard
5 ml (1 tsp)	lemon juice

RAVIGOTE SAUCE
45 ml (3 Tbsp)	white wine vinegar
125 ml (¹/₂ cup)	olive oil
2.5 ml (¹/₂ tsp)	Dijon mustard
5 ml (1 tsp)	onion, finely chopped
5 ml (1 tsp)	capers, finely chopped
15 ml (1 Tbsp)	chopped fines herbes (parsley, chervil, tarragon, chives)
2.5 ml (¹/₂ tsp)	salt

ORIENTAL SAUCE
45 ml (3 Tbsp)	oyster sauce
30 ml (2 Tbsp)	green onion, chopped
45 ml (3 Tbsp)	sake (Japanese rice wine)
30 ml (2 Tbsp)	rice vinegar
2 ml (¹/₂ tsp)	salt

BLACK SAUCE
80 ml (¹/₃ cup)	soy sauce
5 ml (1 tsp)	fresh ginger, chopped
30 ml (2 Tbsp)	red pepper, julienne-cut
15 ml (1 Tbsp)	fresh cilantro, chopped

PREPARATION OF SAUCES
Mix together all the ingredients of each sauce.
Refrigerate.

BEFORE THE MEAL
Preheat oven to 230°C (450°F).
Heat a marble cooking slab for 20 minutes.

PROCEDURE
Debone trout fillets. Cut into small portions. Place on a plate and sprinkle with lemon juice, olive oil and thyme. Marinate for 10 minutes.
Place the marble cooking slab in its holder, and light the heaters.
Season trout with salt and pepper.

PRESENTATION
Each guest cooks trout to taste on the hot marble slab. Serve with the sauces.

"Then — listen! — I see
breath of delighting rise from
those stones the sun touches

and hear a snarl of breath
as a mouth sucks air..."

Margaret Avison

Fennel Cream Soup

Serves 6

POULTRY STOCK

1	onion
1	leek
1	carrot
2 stalks	celery
1 kg (2 lb)	poultry bones
1 ml (¹/₄ tsp)	peppercorns
1 sprig	thyme
2	large fennel bulbs
1	leek (white part only)
45 ml (3 Tbsp)	butter
1 L (4 cups)	chicken stock *or* white stock
2	large potatoes
100 ml (¹/₂ cup)	whipping cream

PREPARATION OF STOCK

Cover onion, leek, carrot, celery stalks and bones with cold water. Add peppercorns and thyme. Bring to a boil. Skim, and simmer for about 2 hours. Pour the stock through a chinois or sieve.

PROCEDURE

Slice fennel and leek. In a saucepan, melt butter and slowly sweat fennel and leek without colouring. When fennel is tender, add stock and diced potatoes. Bring to a boil, simmer for about 30 minutes.

In a blender, purée soup until very smooth. Pass through a fine sieve. Bring to a boil, add cream and season with salt and white pepper.

PRESENTATION

Pour the soup into warm bowls and garnish with feathery green fennel leaves.

"Half-past six on a July morning, and the lake lying in the sun as calm as glass.
The opal colours of the morning light are shot from the surface of the water.
Out on the lake the last thin threads of the mist are clearing away like flecks of cotton wool.
The long call of the loon echoes over the lake. The air is cool and fresh. There is in

Rosemary and Parsley Veal and Trout Phyllo
with Maple Sauce

Serves 4

50 g (¹/₂ cup)	mushrooms, chopped
30 ml (2 Tbsp)	shallot, finely chopped
15 ml (1 Tbsp)	vegetable oil
60 ml (¹/₄ cup)	dry white wine
5 ml (1 tsp)	fresh rosemary, chopped
25 ml (2 Tbsp)	fresh parsley, chopped
80 g (3 oz)	ground veal
10 ml (2 tsp)	vegetable oil
250 g (1 cup)	trout fillets
3 sheets	phyllo pastry
30 ml (2 Tbsp)	butter, melted

MAPLE SAUCE

15 ml (1 Tbsp)	vegetable oil
25 g (2 Tbsp)	shallot, chopped
60 ml (¹/₄ cup)	dry white wine
5 ml (1 tsp)	fresh rosemary
125 ml (¹/₂ cup)	demi-glace
25 ml (2 Tbsp)	light cream
15 ml (1 Tbsp)	maple syrup

GARNISH

15 ml (1 Tbsp)	butter
1	mini zucchini
60 g (¹/₄ cup)	red pepper, diced
25 g (2 Tbsp))	shallot, chopped
15 ml (1 Tbsp)	maple syrup
12	chives

PROCEDURE

Preheat oven to 200°C (400°F).
Sauté mushrooms and shallot in oil, add white wine, rosemary and parsley. Bring to a boil and reduce until almost dry. Sauté ground veal in oil, season with salt and pepper. Add veal to mushrooms and shallot. Cool.
Cut trout fillets into thin slices, season and set aside.
Brush each phyllo pastry sheet with melted butter and spread one over the other. Lay trout slices over three quarters of the surface, and spread the veal mixture over the remaining quarter. Roll, brush with melted butter again and set onto a baking sheet. Place in oven for 10 to 15 minutes, or until pastry turns golden.

PREPARATION OF MAPLE SAUCE

In a small saucepan, sweat chopped shallot in vegetable oil, add white wine and rosemary, bring to a boil and reduce by half. Add demi-glace and simmer one minute. Stir in cream and maple syrup. Season to taste.

PREPARATION OF GARNISH

Sauté mini zucchini, red pepper and shallot in butter, season.

FINAL PREPARATION AND PRESENTATION

Pour sauce onto warm plates, garnish with vegetables and add two thick, diagonally-cut slices of veal and trout phyllo. Garnish with three chives tied together. Add a few drops of maple syrup onto the sauce.

Recipe by Céline Turgeon

Two-Season Lemon and Maple Chicken

Serves 4

Grated rind	of one lemon
500 g (1 lb)	chicken meat, cut in cubes
75 ml (1/4 cup)	lemon juice
75 ml (1/4 cup)	maple syrup
30 ml (2 Tbsp)	olive oil
1 sprig	thyme
30 ml (2 Tbsp)	vegetable oil
1	shallot, chopped
45 ml (3 Tbsp)	white vermouth
100 ml (1/3 cup)	chicken stock
200 ml (3/4 cup)	whipping cream

PREPARATION, 2 HOURS IN ADVANCE
Blanch lemon rind. Set aside.
Mix together lemon juice, maple syrup, olive oil, blanched zests from half a lemon and thyme. Pour on the chicken, stir and refrigerate for 2 hours.

PROCEDURE
Drain chicken cubes and save marinade.
In a frying pan, heat vegetable oil, and fry chicken cubes at moderate heat for 2 minutes. Add chopped shallot and sweat for a few minutes. Add marinade, vermouth, chicken stock and cream. Cook for about 5 minutes or until sauce coats the back of a spoon. Season to taste.

PRESENTATION
Serve the chicken in its sauce on a warm plate. Garnish with seasonal vegetables and a few blanched lemon rind.

Veal Sweetbread and Oyster Mushrooms

Serves 4

500 g (1 lb)	veal sweetbreads
50 g (1/4 cup)	flour
250 g (1/2 lb)	oyster mushrooms
60 g (4 Tbsp)	butter
30 ml (2 Tbsp)	vegetable oil
15 ml (1 Tbsp)	fresh chive, chopped

COURT-BOUILLON

1	carrot
1 stalk	celery
1	small onion
30 ml (2 Tbsp)	white wine vinegar
2 L (8 cups)	water
1 sprig	thyme
1	bay leaf
10	black peppercorns

SAUCE

100 ml (1/2 cup)	dry white wine
1	shallot, finely chopped
1 sprig	thyme
300 ml (1 1/4 cups)	brown stock
100 ml (1/2 cup)	whipping cream

PREPARATION, THE DAY BEFORE
Soak sweetbreads in cold water for 12 hours, changing water regularly until it remains clear.

PREPARATION OF COURT-BOUILLON
Chop carrot, celery and onion.
In a stockpot bring water to a boil, add vegetables, vinegar, thyme, bay leaf and pepper. Simmer for about 20 minutes and cool.

PREPARATION, THE SAME DAY
In a saucepan, cover sweetbreads with cold court-bouillon. Add a little salt. Bring to a boil. Remove sweetbreads, cool under running water and pat dry.
Remove membrane from sweetbreads, place between two plates, add weight on top to press and refrigerate for 1 hour.

PREPARATION OF THE SAUCE
In a saucepan, pour white wine. Add chopped shallot and thyme. Bring to a boil and reduce by two-thirds. Add brown stock and reduce until sauce coats the back of a spoon. Add cream and cook for a few more minutes. Season to taste and pass through a fine sieve. Set aside and keep warm.

PROCEDURE
Keep a few whole oyster mushrooms for garnish, slice the others and sauté in a frying pan with half the butter. Sauté whole mushrooms the same way. Set aside and keep warm.
Slice sweetbreads thinly, season, roll in flour. In a hot frying pan, add remaining butter and vegetable oil. Sauté sweetbreads until golden.

FINAL PREPARATION AND PRESENTATION
In four warm plates, place sliced oyster mushrooms. Add sweetbread slices, pour the sauce. Garnish with the whole oyster mushrooms and chopped fresh chive.

"Laurentian shield
Hidden in wonder and snow, or sudden with summer,
This land stares at the sun in a huge silence
Endlessly repeating something we cannot hear...
It leans away from the world with songs in its lakes
Older than love, and lost in the miles."

F. R. Scott

Fried Fish Platter

Serves 3

FRENCH FRIES
700 g (1¹/₂ lb)	potatoes
450 g (1 lb)	vegetable oil *or* lard

FISH
75 g (¹/₂ cup)	flour *or* bread crumbs
3	walleye *or* other fish, depending on catch
1	lemon

Make a fire with dry wood to get a bed of hot coals; keep wood handy to feed the fire.

PREPARATION OF FRENCH FRIES
Peel potatoes and cut them. Pat dry.
In a large skillet, heat oil or lard and partially fry potatoes. Set aside, keep warm.

PROCEDURE
Fillet the fish. In a bag, mix flour or bread crumbs, salt and pepper to taste. Add fillets and coat completely while shaking.
Place fillets and partially-fried potatoes into hot oil. Do not overcook fish, it should remain flaky, but not dry.

PRESENTATION
Serve immediately with lemon wedges.

Shore lunch

Trout and Scallop Duo
with Grapefruit Beurre Blanc

Serves 4

2	pink grapefruits
50 ml (1/4 cup)	dry white wine
1	shallot
50 ml (1/4 cup)	whipping cream
150 g (5 oz)	semi-salted butter
300 g (10 oz)	trout fillets
300 g (10 oz)	large scallops
250 ml (1 cup)	fish stock

PREPARATION OF GRAPEFRUIT BEURRE BLANC

In a saucepan, squeeze juice from one grapefruit; mix with white wine and finely chopped shallot. Bring to a boil and reduce by half. Add cream and bring to a boil again. Cut cold butter into cubes. Whipping constantly, add to sauce a little at a time. Do not allow sauce to boil, as it could separate. Keep warm.

PROCEDURE

Cut trout fillets into 8 equal pieces.
Slice scallops in two.
Bring fish stock to a boil. Place trout fillets and scallops into stock. Simmer for 2 minutes, remove from heat. Reserve fish stock for later use.

FINAL PREPARATION AND PRESENTATION

Cut second grapefruit into sections.
In the centre of a warm plate, place a layer of scallops. Add a half fillet of trout, a layer of scallops and complete with a final layer of trout. Top with grapefruit beurre blanc. Garnish with grapefruit sections.

Duck Foie Gras au Torchon
with Muscat Jelly from Saint-Jean de Nivernois

Serves 8

650 g (1¹/₂ lb)	duck foie gras
10 g (2 tsp)	salt
4 g (1 tsp)	saltpeter (found in drugstores)
2 g (¹/₂ tsp)	white pepper
30 ml (2 Tbsp)	Cognac

MUSCAT JELLY

250 ml (1 cup)	water
150 ml (²/₃ cup)	Muscat wine
150 g (²/₃ cup)	granulated sugar
14 g (2 packages)	gelatin
15 ml (1 Tbsp)	lemon juice

PREPARATION, 24 HOURS IN ADVANCE
Split foie gras in two, remove main and secondary veins. Mix salt, saltpeter and pepper and season foie gras with this mixture. Sprinkle with Cognac. Macerate in a cool place 30 minutes.

Place foie gras on plastic wrap. Roll tightly to form a cylinder about 8 cm (3 in) in diameter. Tie ends well. Put on a dish cloth, roll up and tie with kitchen string as with a roast.

Fill a large stainless steel pot with water. Do not use aluminum as liver would react with it. Bring water to 95°C (203°F), just under boiling point.

Place foie gras in water and cook for 20 minutes at 95°C (203°F); just under the boiling point. Remove and plunge into a bath of cold water filled with ice to stop the cooking process.

Refrigerate 24 hours before serving. Foie gras can be prepared up to a week in advance.

PREPARATION OF MUSCAT JELLY, 4 HOURS IN ADVANCE
In a saucepan, mix water, wine and sugar. Bring to a boil. Prepare gelatin according to instructions on package. Pour hot wine mixture onto gelatin. Stir well to dissolve, add lemon juice. Pass through a fine sieve. Refrigerate at least 4 hours before serving.

FINAL PREPARATION AND PRESENTATION
Unwrap foie gras and slice with a knife dipped in hot water and dried between each slicing. Serve with Muscat jelly and sourdough bread toasts.

Wrap remaining foie gras in plastic wrap to prevent oxidation. Refrigerate.

Salmon Roulades
with Mushroom Duxelles and Dill Cream Sauce

Serves 4

250 g (¹/₂ lb)	mushrooms
30 ml (2 Tbsp)	shallot, chopped
60 ml (¹/₄ cup)	dry white wine
30 ml (2 Tbsp)	whipping cream
600 g (1 lb 6 oz)	salmon fillets
45 ml (3 Tbsp)	olive oil

SAUCE
250 ml (1 cup)	dry white wine
45 ml (3 Tbsp)	shallot, chopped
250 ml (1 cup)	fish stock
250 ml (1 cup)	fresh dill, chopped
125 ml (¹/₂ cup)	whipping cream

PREPARATION OF DUXELLES
Chop mushrooms finely. Place in a saucepan, with shallot and wine. Cook gently until liquid has evaporated. Season with salt and pepper and add cream. Cool.

PREPARATION OF ROULADE
Cut salmon fillets to a thickness such that it can be rolled up.
Spread duxelles on salmon, roll it up and tie with kitchen string every 2 cm (1 in) to keep the shape. Refrigerate to handle more easily.

PREPARATION OF THE SAUCE
In a saucepan, pour white wine, add shallots, and reduce by half. Add fish stock and fresh dill and simmer 5 minutes. Add cream and reduce a few minutes. In a blender, purée sauce. Pour back into saucepan, and reduce to desired consistency. Season with salt and pepper.

PROCEDURE
Cut roulade into sections, between string ties.
In a non-stick frying pan, heat olive oil. Put roulades in pan and cook about 2 minutes. Gently turn over roulades and cook another minute. Salmon should be slightly pink inside to keep it tender and juicy.

PRESENTATION
Pour the dill sauce in a warm plate. Place assorted vegetables around plate, with roulade in centre. Garnish with sprig of fresh dill.

"shall I go to heaven or a-fishing?"

Henry David Thoreau

Warm Chicken Liver Salad
with Vinaigre Royal from L'Île d'Orléans

Serves 4

150 g (5 oz)	mesclun (mixture of mild and bitter salad greens)
1	leek, white part
1	carrot
1	endive
15 ml (1 Tbsp)	fresh chive, chopped
350 g (13 oz)	chicken livers
120 ml (¹/₂ cup)	olive oil
30 ml (2 Tbsp)	shallot, chopped
60 ml (¹/₄ cup)	Four Fruit Vinaigre Royal from l'Île d'Orléans
FOR GARNISH	strawberries, raspberries, blueberries

PROCEDURE
Rinse mesclun, pat dry and place in a bowl.
Julienne-cut carrot and leek. Break endive into leaves, then slice lengthwise thinly. Add to mesclun with fresh chive. Clean, trim and cut chicken livers into big pieces. In a frying pan, heat 30 ml (2 Tbsp) olive oil. Sauté liver and add chopped shallot. Deglaze with Four Fruit vinegar, add remaining oil. Adjust seasoning.

PRESENTATION
Place warm livers and cooking vinaigrette onto salad. Garnish with strawberries, raspberries and blueberries.

"The Song My Paddle Sings

August is laughing across the sky,   The river rolls in its rocky bed;   And up on the hills, against the sky,
Laughing while paddle, canoe and I,   My paddle is plying its way ahead;   A fir tree rocking its lullaby,
Drift, drift,   Dip, dip,   Swings, swings,
Where the hills uplift   While the waters flip   Its emerald wings,
On either side of the current swift.   In foam as over their breast we slip...   Swelling the song that my paddle sings."

Pauline Johnson

To explore...

Lake Saint-Jean Wananish in Court-bouillon
with Garden Sorrel Sauce

COURT-BOUILLON

2	carrots
1	onion
30 ml (2 Tbsp)	olive oil
3 L (12 cups)	cold water
250 ml (1 cup)	white wine vinegar
30 ml (2 Tbsp)	salt
1 sprig	fresh thyme
1	bay leaf
3 sprigs	fresh parsley
10	peppercorns
1.5 kg (3 lb)	wananish (landlocked salmon) salmon *or* trout
2 ml (¹/2 tsp)	white pepper

SORREL SAUCE

125 ml (¹/2 cup)	dry white wine
1	shallot
375 ml (1¹/2 cups)	fresh sorrel
250 ml (1 cup)	fish stock *or* court-bouillon
250 ml (1 cup)	whipping cream

PREPARATION OF COURT-BOUILLON, THE DAY BEFORE

Peel and chop carrots and onion. In a saucepan, sweat carrots and onion in olive oil. Add cold water, white wine vinegar, salt, thyme, bay leaf, parsley and peppercorns. Bring to a boil and simmer 20 minutes. Pour court-bouillon through a sieve and cool.

PROCEDURE

Scale the wananish. Season the inside with salt and white pepper. Place in a fish kettle or a large pan with a tightly-fitting lid. Pour in cold court-bouillon.

Bring to a gentle boil and simmer 10 minutes. Fish should remain flaky but not dry.
Remove from heat and let stand 5 minutes.

PREPARATION OF THE SORREL SAUCE

In a saucepan, pour white wine and add finely chopped shallot. Bring to a boil and reduce the wine by half.
Add sorrel leaves, fish stock or court-bouillon and cream. Reduce sauce for a few minutes, then purée in a blender until smooth. Through a sieve, pour back into saucepan. Bring to a boil, season to taste and reduce until sauce coats the back of a spoon. If sauce becomes too thick, add fish stock or court-bouillon.

FINAL PREPARATION AND PRESENTATION

Remove fish from court-bouillon and place on a warm serving platter. Serve with sorrel sauce and steamed potatoes.

Blinis
with Trout Caviar

3 dozen blinis

TROUT CAVIAR

250 ml (1 cup)	trout eggs (before spawning)
30 ml (2 Tbsp)	unrefined salt
10 g (1¼ package)	dry yeast
5 ml (1 tsp)	granulated sugar
200 ml (¾ cup)	lukewarm water
200 g (1¾ cups)	flour
50 g (⅓ cup)	buckwheat flour
325 ml (1⅓ cups)	lukewarm milk
2	egg yolks
30 ml (2 Tbsp)	melted butter
5 ml (1 tsp)	salt
2	egg whites
50 ml (¼ cup)	vegetable oil
15 g (1 Tbsp)	butter
150 ml (⅔ cup)	whipping cream
	ground pepper
10 ml (2 tsp)	vodka
120 ml (4 oz)	caviar

To discover...

ADVANCE PREPARATION OF THE CAVIAR
Wash the trout eggs, dry and sprinkle with salt. Place in a covered dish in the refrigerator for 4 hours. Stir occasionally. Rinse trout eggs and place in a jar. Refrigerate immediately. Caviar will easily keep for 2 weeks.

PREPARATION OF THE BLINIS, AT LEAST 6 HOURS IN ADVANCE
The dough can be prepared a day in advance.
Dissolve yeast and sugar in lukewarm water. Add 2 to 3 spoonfuls of flour, mix and let the leaven for 15 minutes in a warm place.
In a bowl, add the remaining flour with two-thirds of the buckwheat flour, and mix. Dig a small well in the centre, pour in half the milk and the leaven. Whisk vigorously until the dough is smooth. Cover the bowl with a cloth and let the dough rise for three hours in a warm place. Beat well, adding the rest of the buckwheat flour. Let rise for two hours.

Beat again while slowly adding the remaining milk, the egg yolks, melted butter and salt. Beat the egg whites until they form stiff peaks, and fold carefully in the dough. Let rest for 30 minutes.

PROCEDURE
Heat a frying pan. Add a small amount of oil. Pour the dough one small ladle at a time and cook the blinis until golden brown on both sides.
Brush with melted butter. Keep warm.
Whip cream, season with pepper and add a few drops of vodka.

PRESENTATION
Place the blinis on a hot serving platter. Serve with cream, caviar and iced vodka!

Trout Mousseline in a Brioche
with Beurre Blanc

Serves 8

TROUT MOUSSELINE

225 g (1 cup)	deboned trout meat
250 ml (1 cup)	whipping cream
5 ml (1 tsp)	salt
1 pinch	white pepper
1/2 package	fresh spinach

BRIOCHE DOUGH

5 g (1 1/4 tsp)	dry yeast
100 ml (7 Tbsp)	water
1 ml (1/4 tsp)	granulated sugar
250 g (1 3/4 cups)	flour
2 ml (1/2 tsp)	salt
4	eggs
125 g (1/2 cup)	unsalted butter (at room temperature)

BEURRE BLANC

1	shallot, chopped
175 ml (3/4 cup)	fish stock
125 ml (1/2 cup)	white wine vinegar
125 g (1/2 cup)	unsalted butter
15 ml (1 Tbsp)	whipping cream
5 ml (1 tsp)	salt
1 pinch	white pepper

PREPARATION OF TROUT MOUSSELINE, 12 HOURS IN ADVANCE

In a food processor, purée trout meat. Add whipping cream in a thin, steady stream. Do not mix too much, so as not to whip cream. Add salt and pepper. Remove mixture from food processor and pass through a sieve. Refrigerate 1 hour.

On a piece of plastic wrap, pour a length of mousse. Roll the wrap to form a cylinder approximately 5 cm (1 1/2 in) in diameter. Tie both ends securely with kitchen string. Refrigerate.

Fill a large pot with water. Bring to a boil. Place mousseline roll in water. Simmer for 15 minutes. Remove and cool, then refrigerate. Keep water for spinach. Wash spinach and remove stems. Blanch in boiling water and remove immediately. Drain and cool spinach.

PREPARATION OF BRIOCHE DOUGH, 2 HOURS IN ADVANCE

Dissolve dry yeast and sugar in lukewarm water. Add 2 to 3 spoons of flour, mix and set aside in a warm place for 15 minutes.

In a bowl, mix remaining flour, salt, 3 eggs and yeast mixture. Knead dough for 10 minutes. Cover and allow to rise for 1 hour in a warm place. Break up dough and add butter while kneading by hand.

PROCEDURE

Roll dough into a rectangle. Cover with a layer of spinach leaves. Unwrap trout mousseline and place in the centre of the dough. Brush dough edges with beaten egg. Carefully roll dough around trout mousseline. Place on a buttered pastry tray or in a bread pan, approximately 20 cm x 12 cm (9 in x 5 in). Cover with a cloth and allow dough to rise for 30 minutes.

Preheat oven to 190°C (375°F). Brush dough with mixture of egg, salt and water. Bake for 40 minutes.

PREPARATION OF BEURRE BLANC

In a thick bottom saucepan, pour fish stock, white wine vinegar and add chopped shallot. Bring to a boil and reduce by half. Cut cold butter into cubes. Over low heat, add butter cubes, one at a time, while whisking mixture. Add cream, season to taste, and pass through a sieve. Keep sauce warm, but do not boil, or it may separate.

FINAL PREPARATION AND PRESENTATION

Slice brioche with a serrated knife. Place on warm plates. Serve with beurre blanc.

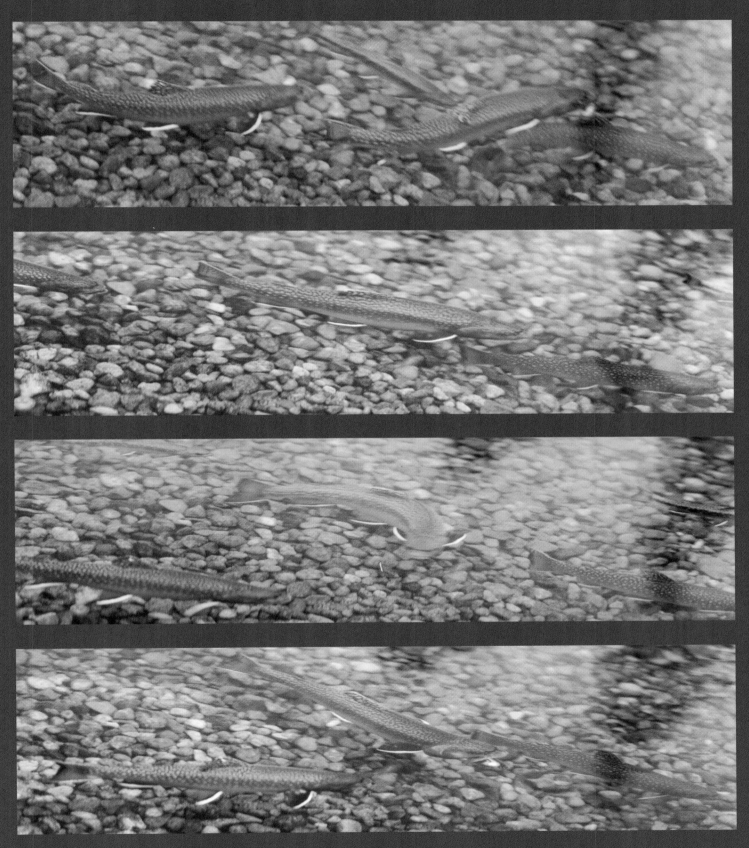

Trout on spawning grounds

Roast Monkfish
with Celery and Lime

Serves 4

900 g (2 lb)	monkfish
45 ml (3 Tbsp)	olive oil

CELERY AND LIME SAUCE

30 ml (2 Tbsp)	shallot, finely chopped
80 ml (¹/₃ cup)	dry white wine
1	lime
125 ml (¹/₂ cup)	celery, finely diced
500 ml (2 cups)	fish stock
80 ml (¹/₃ cup)	whipping cream

PREPARATION OF MONKFISH
Remove skin and backbone. Tie monkfish with string as you would a roast. Season with salt and pepper.

PREPARATION OF SAUCE
Zest lime and extract juice.
In a small saucepan, pour lime juice, white wine and add shallot. Bring to a boil. Reduce by half. Add diced celery and fish stock. Bring to a boil, and simmer for 20 minutes. In a blender, purée sauce. Pass through a fine sieve. Pour back into saucepan, add cream. Bring to a boil and reduce for 2 minutes. Add lime zest. Set aside and keep warm.

PROCEDURE
Preheat oven to 160°C (325°F).
In a frying pan, heat olive oil. Sear monkfish roast on all sides. Place in oven for 10 minutes. Remove roast from oven, cover with aluminum foil and let stand for 5 minutes.

FINAL PREPARATION AND PRESENTATION
Cut roast into thick slices. Place on warm plates and top with the sauce.

"This land like a mirror turns you inward
        And you become a forest in a furtive lake;
The dark pines of your mind reach downward,
    you dream in the green of your time,
        your memory is a row of sinking pines."

Gwendolyn MacEwen

The trophy from Lake Coburn

A story as told by Dave Boulet

The territory of the lodge at Lake Portage has four lakes, including Lake Coburn, a trophy fish lake. Coburn is a small, 30-hectare, headwater lake, at the deepest point some ten metres deep. The water is crystal clear and the bottom rocky. Neither algae nor cattails interfere with a fly fisher's casts. Here anglers are joined by loons or even, occasionally, a moose.

True, like all fish stories, this one relates events that occurred circa 1997.

Trophy speckled and rainbow trout, weighing between one and five pounds, swim in Lake Coburn's waters. To maintain the fishing quality the daily limit is two per person. Management needs an iron fist to enforce the quotas on this lake...

That summer an important real estate developer from the Montreal region, Mr. Wayne, generously invited a group of friends to join him at Portage. By the last day of the trip all his friends had done very well, and only four fish were left to be caught... naturally on Lake Coburn. The angler in question was none other than Mr. Wayne himself, accompanied by a friend.

The pair hadn't caught a single fish. They wanted to cast, being inveterate fly fishers who will only use a fly when fishing. We urged them to use a "sinking silk line" (which doesn't float) and to troll their lines. But Lake Coburn is very difficult to fish when it isn't windy, because you have to cast far away from the boat. The fish are big and fierce, and the water is so clear that even in seven metres of water, you can see the fish at the end of the line...

For about ten days the guides had been trolling successfully with a black Woolly Bugger and a silver-bodied Muddler Minnow. However, each day Mr. Wayne and his friend insist on casting their flies. The boss was getting a little testy and complained, "What's going on? I'm paying for this trip but I'm not catching any fish. Open a trap and put more in!"

For the last day I decided to be their guide. Mr. Wayne issued me an ultimatum, "We're leaving tomorrow morning. We'll give you an hour to put us into fish on Coburn or else we'll go catch the four fish in Lake Champagne." (Note to reader: the fish in Champagne are smaller, but easy to catch.)

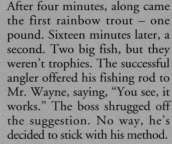

So I offered the boss a proposition, "If you catch your four fish in an hour, do you agree to buy another visit here next year?" He agreed. Stopwatch in hand, the three of us headed out onto the lake. Mr. Wayne's friend agreed to use the sinking line and his soon-to-be-famous fly. Mr. Wayne insisted on sticking with his floating line.

After four minutes, along came the first rainbow trout – one pound. Sixteen minutes later, a second. Two big fish, but they weren't trophies. The successful angler offered his fishing rod to Mr. Wayne, saying, "You see, it works." The boss shrugged off the suggestion. No way, he's decided to stick with his method.

After 43 minutes the third trout came to the sinking line, and once again Mr. Wayne was offered the rod. Now there's only one fish left to fill the limit.

Finally, the boss accepted the rod. We kept trolling and at the 56th minute a trout grabbed the fly. The rod bent and the fish rose from the bottom. The rainbow trout – here we call it a poor man's salmon – had lots of fight in him, jumping five times clear of the surface. The fish had taken the fly about 25 metres behind the boat and nine minutes passed before it was finally reeled-in.

The men soon understood why the battle had been so spirited: the rainbow measured 23 and 3/4 inches and weighed 5 and 3/4 pounds. It was the biggest fish ever caught at the club. I cut off the fly and offered it to Mr. Wayne. He pinned it on my vest, saying, "It's now a piece of history." It's still on my vest by the way.

The next day, when it was time to leave, Mr. Wayne, always a gentleman, announced, "I think a beautiful fish like this belongs more to the club than the angler." So the trout was mounted and Mr. Wayne's name placed on the souvenir plaque.

Goose hunting in high winds

A story as told by Philippe Tanguay

It was late autumn, near the end of the hunting season, and the tides at Cap Tourmente were wicked. Jacques Cartier named it Cap Tourmentine and it's not without reason that it bears either name. The cape juts out into the Saint Lawrence River, and when the winds are from the east things shake. But when the winds come from the west all is calm because you're at the bottom of La Miche hill below the mountain of the Côte de Beaupré. Saint Joachim, on Cap Tourmente, was the site of one of North America's earliest farms. The intervale was flat and clear of trees, thus easy for the settler's to cultivate. That original farm is still standing and you can visit it.

That autumn day there were strong easterly winds; it was hell. I had acquired a Quebec City carriage horse; a real beauty – well-muscled and in good shape. It was my second horse of the season. The first had almost died along the tidal flats. It's very demanding on a horse, because it's always up to its knees in mud, and hauling: clients, guns, decoys, geese. The sleigh is always heavy.

I was off onto the tidal flat with that horse. It was windy, very windy; raining and hailing as well. The wind was driving the rain and hail into our faces so hard it hurt. I had trouble seeing ahead of me. Unable to see what was ahead, the horse was skittish too. The ice and the water got into its eyes making it hard to control. Like I said, it was hell.

Out on the flat was a guy who had brought decoys, just silhouettes. The silhouettes, the shells, the decoys, everything was being carried off by the wind.

With the wind blowing a gale, not a goose was passing. They had stayed on the islands, such as Isle aux Grues, and sandbars in the middle of the river. They were too smart to fly. The winds were surely gusting to 100 kilometres an hour. It was blowing like crazy!

We didn't stay long in the blind. I said to my sports, 'let's get a move on fast, the tide comes in a lot quicker when the wind is from the east.' The strong east wind meant not only a higher than normal tide but one that would rise rapidly, almost as fast as a man can walk. First it fills the river channel, but as soon as it reaches the flat it floods almost immediately. You've got to be quick.

We had to secure the blinds which are dug into the silt. Usually, that's the guide's job, but this time I asked the clients to help because I had to hold on to one very unhappy horse. Now, I try not to swear, but that day the odd curse did slip out. My horse wouldn't listen to reason. And when a horse won't listen, it really won't listen. It was tense and just wanted to bolt. The situation was becoming frightening.

The clients were nervous too, you could tell because there wasn't a lot of talk in the sleigh. One gentleman left half of his decoys behind. When we turned toward the intervale, the horse got excited and took off in a flash. After all, it knows the route. On the way out to the blinds it sees the riverbank and knows that we're near the flats; so it knows when we're headed back as well.

What frightened me the most was that the tidal flat is criss-crossed with little creeks that carry off the last of the saltwater when the tide recedes. When you

cross these tiny rivers you don't stop, but you slow down and go gently down one side and up the other. But with this horse, on this day, there was no slowing down. So when we hit a little stream, everything in the sleigh flew up, just like when a boat hits a wave. I had trouble stopping the horse when we got to the camp. All in all it was quite the ride, and quite the day. I did get a good tip though – and believe it was well-deserved.

Lake Portage
Porterhouse Roast

Serves 8

2.5 kg (5¹/₂ lb)	beef *or* moose porterhouse (whole T-bone) trimmed, deboned and tied along with the bone with kitchen string
125 g (¹/₂ cup)	butter, at room temperature
30 ml (2 Tbsp)	Dijon mustard
2.5 ml (¹/₂ tsp)	rosemary
8	potatoes
30 ml (2 Tbsp)	vegetable oil

SAUCE

250 ml (1 cup)	dry red wine
1	shallot, chopped
500 ml (2 cups)	demi-glace *or* brown stock

Ask butcher to prepare roast as desired. Pat dry meat. Preheat oven to 260°C (500°F).

PROCEDURE

Mix butter, mustard and rosemary and brush meat with mixture. In a roasting pan, place roast and cook 20 minutes. Reduce temperature to 135°C (275°F).

Brush potatoes with oil and place around roast. Continue cooking 45 minutes for rare meat; 1 hour for medium. For best results, use meat thermometer: 55°C (131°F) for rare; 62°C (144°F) for medium; 68° to 70°C (154° to 158°F) for well-done. Temperature should be taken from centre of meat.

Once cooked, remove roast and potatoes and place on serving platter. Cover with aluminum foil.

PREPARATION OF THE SAUCE

Skim off the fat. Put roasting pan on stovetop over high heat. Deglaze with red wine, add shallot and reduce by half. Add demi-glace or brown stock. Reduce until sauce has a good coating consistency. Pass sauce through a sieve and pour into a gravy boat.

PRESENTATION

Bring serving platter to table. First slice the fillet for the ladies and then the sirloin. Serve on very hot plates with the potatoes and a cauliflower au gratin.

"Hemlock and aspen, chestnut, beech, and fir
Go tiering down storm-worn crest and ledge,
While in the hollows of the dark ravine
See the red road emerge, then disappear
Towards the wide plain and fertile valley lands."

Bliss Carman

Shrimp and Scallop Strudel
with Spinach

Serves 6

1 package	fresh spinach
200 g (1¹/₂ cups)	Nordic shrimps
10 ml (2 tsp)	whiskey
240 g (1 cup)	salted butter
10	scallops, size 20/30
15 sheets (³/₄ pkg)	phyllo pastry
15 ml (1 Tbsp)	poppy seeds
1	egg yolk

PROCEDURE

Preheat oven to 180°C (350°F).

Wash spinach well, pat dry and remove stems. Chop in food processor for 1 minute. Set aside.

Chop shrimps in food processor for 1 minute. Add shrimps, whiskey and 120 g (¹/₂ cup) melted butter to spinach. Season with salt and pepper. Mix well. Remove side muscle from scallops and cut into thick slices. Melt remaining butter. Brush 12 phyllo sheets with melted butter, laying one on top of the other. Add 3 phyllo sheets without butter.

Spread spinach mixture on phyllo pastry. Place chopped scallops on spinach mixture, and roll up in strudel style. Place on a cooking sheet covered with parchment paper.

Brush strudel with egg yolk and sprinkle with poppy seeds. Bake in oven for 45 minutes, or until pastry is golden.

Recipe by Véronique Gosselin

Lake Portage
Tuna Burger

Serves 4

170 g (6 oz)	canned tuna
80 ml (1/3 cup)	rolled oats
30 ml (2 Tbsp)	raisins
80 ml (1/3 cup)	unsalted pistachios, chopped
15 ml (1 Tbsp)	sesame seeds
1	egg, lightly beaten
120 ml (1/2 cup)	grated Emmental *or* Mozzarella cheese
80 ml (1/3 cup)	prunes, chopped
30 ml (2 Tbsp)	butter *or* vegetable oil

PROCEDURE

Drain tuna. Mix all ingredients. Form into patties. In a frying pan, cook 3 to 4 minutes on each side.

PRESENTATION

Serve on a bun with a spinach and onion salad.

Recipe by Véronique Gosselin

"A blazing camp-fire late at night, beneath a sky luminous with more stars than the mind could comfortably conjure: nature's way, you think, of dwarfing the human imagination, not into insignificance but into a proper perspective of its place in the larger world..."

Neil Bissoondath

Chicken Stuffed with Scallop Mousse
Mango Sauce

Serves 4

250 g (¹/₂ lb)	scallops
170 ml (³/₄ cup)	whipping cream
5 ml (1 tsp)	salt
1 pinch	white pepper
125 ml (¹/₂ cup)	Ricotta cheese
1	small red cabbage
2	boneless chicken breasts

MANGO SAUCE

125 ml (¹/₂ cup)	dry white wine
45 ml (3 Tbsp)	shallot, finely chopped
250 ml (1 cup)	chicken stock
1	mango, peeled and cubed
60 ml (4 Tbsp)	whipping cream

PREPARATION, A FEW HOURS IN ADVANCE

In a food processor, purée scallops. Add cream, salt and pepper. Continue to blend for a few seconds. Transfer into a bowl and add Ricotta cheese. Cover and refrigerate.

PROCEDURE

Choose the best leaves from the cabbage. Blanch in a large pot of boiling salted water. Remove and cool under cold running water. Set aside.

Place chicken breasts between two layers of plastic wrap. Beat with a mallet to thin. Spread chicken breasts on another layer of plastic wrap. Season with salt and pepper. Cover with one or two cabbage leaves. Spread scallop stuffing evenly on leaves. Roll in plastic wrap.

In a pot filled with boiling water, place stuffed chicken breasts. Simmer for 15 minutes. Remove from water and cool for a few minutes.

PREPARATION OF THE SAUCE

In a saucepan, pour white wine, add chopped shallot and bring to a boil. Reduce by half. Add chicken stock and mango cubes. Cook at low heat for 10 minutes. In a blender, purée sauce. Pour back into saucepan. Add cream and bring to a boil. Season with salt and pepper. Set aside and keep warm.

FINAL PREPARATION AND PRESENTATION

Unwrap chicken breasts, slice and place on warm plates. Serve with mango sauce.

"*I am the land that listens, I am the land that broods;*
steeped in eternal beauty, chrystaline waters and woods"

Robert W. Service

"The loon has left its voice
and flown away.
I hear it in the early light
and just before sleeping,
rolling through reeds toward the shore.

It lives in the lake
and sometimes in the mind.
Now it sits on the belly
of a rainbow trout
  moving like memory through darkness."

Lorna Crozier

Pheasant Suprême
Maple Sabayon and Caramelized Apples

Serves 2

2	pheasant suprêmes (breasts)
15 ml (1 Tbsp)	vegetable oil

SABAYON

60 ml (¹/₄ cup)	apple cider vinegar
60 ml (¹/₄ cup)	maple syrup
60 ml (¹/₄ cup)	dry white wine
1	shallot, chopped
1	egg yolk

CARAMELIZED APPLES

¹/₂	apple
10 ml (2 tsp)	butter
1 pinch	granulated sugar

PROCEDURE

Preheat oven to 180°C (350°F).
Season pheasant breasts with salt and pepper. In a frying pan, heat oil and sear on both sides. Place in oven for 10 minutes to complete cooking.

PREPARATION OF SABAYON

In a saucepan, mix cider vinegar, maple syrup, white wine and shallot. Bring to a boil and reduce by half to concentrate flavours. Pour mixture through a sieve and set aside to cool.
In the top part of a bain-marie, mix egg yolk with the cider vinegar, maple syrup and white wine reduction. Place on the bottom part of the bain-marie containing boiling water, whisk sabayon vigorously until thick and unctuous. Season.

PREPARATION OF CARAMELIZED APPLES

Peel apple, cut into wedges and core. In a frying pan, heat butter and sauté apple wedges until tender. Sprinkle with sugar and complete cooking.

FINAL PREPARATION AND PRESENTATION

Cut suprêmes into thin slices and place on warm plates. Top with sabayon and garnish with caramelized apple wedges.

Recipe by Sonia Ratté

Braised Guinea Fowl Suprêmes
with Wild Aromas

Serves 8

200 g (¹/₂ lb)	wild mushrooms
100 g (¹/₂ cup)	pearl onions
100 g (3 oz)	bacon, unsliced
250 ml (1 cup)	dry red wine
250 ml (1 cup)	brown veal stock
1 sprig	fresh thyme
8	Guinea fowl suprêmes (breasts)
125 ml (¹/₂ cup)	whipping cream

PREPARATION

Rapidly clean, brush and wash mushrooms under cold running water. Pat dry, then chop finely.
Poach mushrooms in 250 ml (1 cup) boiling water, for about 5 minutes. Drain, and keep cooking juices.
Cut bacon into small chunks.

PROCEDURE

In a deep saucepan, sauté pearl onions and bacon until golden brown. Deglaze with red wine, veal stock and mushrooms with a bit of their cooking juices. Add thyme and reduce by half.
Pour sauce into a bowl. Set aside.
In the saucepan, sear Guinea fowl suprêmes at high heat on all sides. Add sauce, reduce heat and simmer 7 to 10 minutes. Remove suprêmes from saucepan. Set aside, keep warm.

FINAL PREPARATION AND PRESENTATION

Add cream to sauce. Reduce for a few minutes and adjust seasoning. Serve Guinea fowl suprêmes with the sauce.

Recipe by Patrick Rioual

Beet and Rutabaga
Concerto

Serves 12

1 kg (2 lb)	beets
5 ml (1 tsp)	white vinegar
1	large rutabaga
60 g (¹/₄ cup)	butter
1	large Spanish onion
3 stalks	celery
1	leek
3 L (12 cups)	chicken stock
1	bay leaf
15 ml (1 Tbsp)	oregano
15 ml (1 Tbsp)	parsley

PREPARATION
Peel the beets, cook in water and white vinegar for 45 minutes, or until tender.

PROCEDURE
Peel the rutabaga and cut in small pieces. Slice the other vegetables.

In a saucepan, melt 30 g (¹/₈ cup) butter. Sweat half the onion, celery, rutabaga and the white part of the leek. Add one litre (4 cups) of chicken stock and herbs. Salt and pepper to taste. Simmer 20 minutes. Once cooked, purée in a blender.

When beets are cooked, remove from water and sweat in butter with remaining onion and the green part of the leek. Add one litre (4 cups) of chicken stock. Salt and pepper to taste. Simmer 5 minutes. Once cooked, purée in a blender.

FINAL PREPARATION AND PRESENTATION
Since the secret of success is to have the same consistency for the two soups, use remaining chicken stock to adjust consistency. Using two pitchers, pour soups simultaneously in warm bowls.
Decorate.

Recipe by Véronique Gosselin

"I hear faint music in the solitudes;
A dreamlike melody that whispers peace
Imbues the calmy forest, and sweet rills

Of pensive feeling murmur through my brain,
Like ripplings of pure water down the hills..."

Charles Sangster

Duck Magret
with Honey and Blueberries

Serves 4

2	duck magrets *or* snow goose breasts

BLUEBERRY SAUCE

45 ml (3 Tbsp)	blueberry honey
45 ml (3 Tbsp)	balsamic vinegar
1	shallot
300 ml (1¼ cups)	stock from duck *or* goose *or* commercial demi-glace
125 ml (½ cup)	fresh blueberries

PREPARATION

Score the skin of duck magrets in a grid pattern, without cutting through to the meat. Season with salt and pepper. Brush goose breasts with their own fat.

PREPARATION OF BLUEBERRY SAUCE

In a small saucepan, pour honey and cook for about 2 minutes. Add balsamic vinegar and finely chopped shallot and cook for another minute. Reduce stock by half. Add stock to honey mixture along with blueberries. Cook a few minutes until sauce coats the back of a spoon. Season to taste. Set aside and keep warm.

PROCEDURE

Preheat oven to 180°C (350°F).
Place a non-stick frying pan over high heat without using oil. When very hot, sear magrets on both sides, starting on skin side. Place in oven. Bake for about 5 minutes, or until meat is pink. Remove from oven and cover with aluminum foil.

FINAL PREPARATION AND PRESENTATION

Let rest for 5 minutes before cutting magrets. Place slices on warm plates, cover with sauce and serve with vegetables such as baby buttered cattails.

Cattails are edible early in the season. While it is still hidden in its stem, ready to bloom, one breaks the stem where it is slightly swollen and a little green to remove the baby cattail. It is eaten boiled or sautéed in butter.

Deny Mc Donald - Taxidermist

Duckling
with Seasonal Berries

Serves 4

1	2 kg (4.4 lb) duckling
125 ml (¹/₂ cup)	whipping cream
125 ml (¹/₂ cup)	dried cranberries
30 ml (2 Tbsp)	vegetable oil

BERRY SAUCE
30 ml (2 Tbsp)	shallot, chopped
125 ml (¹/₂ cup)	dry red wine
125 ml (¹/₂ cup)	cranberry juice
500 ml (2 cups)	duck stock
60 ml (¹/₄ cup)	physalis (ground cherries), quartered
60 ml (¹/₄ cup)	fresh cranberries

PREPARATION

Debone duck, without removing breast skin. Keep bones to make stock.

In a food processor, purée meat from thighs and drumsticks. Add whipping cream and continue puréeing for a few seconds. Add dried cranberries, season with salt and pepper.

PROCEDURE

Make an incision in the suprême, opening like a wallet. Season the inside and stuff. Close cavity and tie with string. Preheat oven to 180°C (350°F).

In a frying pan, heat oil. Sear suprême on both sides. Place in oven skin side down and complete cooking for 20 minutes or until meat temperature reaches 70-72°C (158-162°F).

PREPARATION OF THE SAUCE

Remove suprême from frying pan. Drain excess fat. Sweat shallot. Deglaze with red wine and cranberry juice and reduce by half. Add duck stock and reduce by half again. Adjust consistency if needed with a beurre manié (mixture of butter and flour). Pass sauce through a chinois or a sieve and adjust seasoning. Add fresh berries, and heat slightly.

FINAL PREPARATION AND PRESENTATION

Slice duck suprême, and place on warm plates, with the seasonal berry sauce.

Recipe by Jean-Félix Giguère

Hare or Partridge
Pithiviers

Serves 4

1	hare *or* 2 partridges
30 ml (2 Tbsp)	vegetable oil
100 ml (1/2 cup)	carrots, finely chopped
50 ml (1/4 cup)	celery, finely chopped
50 ml (1/4 cup)	onion, finely chopped
15 ml (1 Tbsp)	juniper berries, crushed
100 ml (1/2 cup)	dry red wine
100 ml (1/2 cup)	brown stock *or* beef broth
100 ml (1/2 cup)	demi-glace
50 g (2 oz)	triple cream Brie cheese
30 ml (2 Tbsp)	fresh parsley, chopped

SAUCE

250 ml (1 cup)	demi-glace
15 g (1 Tbsp)	butter
15 ml (1 Tbsp)	flour
250 g (8 oz)	puff pastry
1	egg, beaten

PREPARATION OF GAME
Preheat oven to 135°C (275°F).
Cut game meat into pieces. In a saucepan, heat oil. Sear game pieces on all sides. Add carrots, celery, onion, half the crushed juniper berries, red wine and beef stock. Bring to a boil, cover and cook in oven for an hour. Cool and debone. Set meat aside.

PROCEDURE
Pour cooking juices through a sieve, add demi-glace, the remaining juniper berries and reduce until sauce coats the back of a spoon.
Chop meat into large chunks, add Brie cut into small cubes, parsley and a few tablespoons of sauce to moisten. Adjust seasoning.

PREPARATION OF BROWN ROUX
Mix butter and flour, cook over low heat until flour browns.

PREPARATION OF THE SAUCE
Dilute brown roux with demi-glace. Cook on low heat, stirring constantly until mixture thickens. Simmer for 1 hour.

FINAL PREPARATION
Roll out puff pastry to about 3 mm (1/8 in). Cut out four circles 15 cm (6 in) and four 20 cm (8 in) in diameter. On the smaller pastries, place meat stuffing. Brush the edge of the pastry with an egg wash glaze (a mixture of beaten egg, water and salt). Cover with a larger circle of puff pastry. Seal together and place in a roasting pan. Brush tops of pithiviers with egg wash glaze. Refrigerate a few hours before cooking.
Preheat oven to 180°C (350°F). Pour a few drops of water in the pan. Bake for about 20 minutes.

PRESENTATION
Place pithivier on a warm plate, pour a bit of sauce around and garnish.

"I sat so still that a rabbit sprinted past not twenty feet in front of me, and a minute later, right at my feet, there was the breathlike shadow of a pursuing owl."

Sinclair Ross

Roast Pork Loin
with a Citrus Glaze

Serves 6

800 g (1³/₄ lb)	pork loin, deboned and trimmed
1	lemon
1	grapefruit
2	oranges
45 ml (3 Tbsp)	vegetable oil
1 sprig	fresh rosemary
30 ml (2 Tbsp)	icing sugar
30 ml (2 Tbsp)	Cognac

PREPARATION, 24 HOURS IN ADVANCE

Trim all visible fat from pork loin.

Squeeze juice from half a lemon, half a grapefruit, and one and a half oranges. Place the loin in a large freezer bag and pour in citrus juice. Seal bag, removing as much air as possible. Refrigerate and marinate for 24 hours. Rotate regularly.

PROCEDURE

Drain, saving citrus juice. Pat dry meat. Salt and pepper. Preheat oven to 180°C (350°F).

In a roasting pan, heat vegetable oil. At medium-high heat, sear meat on all sides.

Cut remaining half lemon, half grapefruit and half orange into slices of about ¹/₂ cm (¹/₄ in). Place in roasting pan with pork loin and rosemary. Cook in oven.

Mix citrus marinade with icing sugar and Cognac. During cooking, regularly baste roast with this mixture. When roast reaches 65°C (150°F) when tested with a meat thermometer in the center of the meat, remove from oven and cover with aluminum foil for 10 minutes. Cooking time should be about 45 minutes. Pork is best served slightly pink.

FINAL PREPARATION AND PRESENTATION

Slice roast pork loin and deglaze roasting pan. Place on a warm serving plate. Pour cooking juices and garnish with slices of citrus fruit.

"...look towards the river to know the waterfalls, the water's rhythm, its violence and peace, the lulls of time, the law that works for them and the thousands-of-years-old gold from the sun that gives us the round of the seasons, our own fortune."

Robert Lalonde

Partridge
with Apple and Cabbage

Serves 8

1	medium cabbage
125 g (4 oz)	lean salt pork
1	medium onion
1	clove
1	bouquet garni
250 ml (1 cup)	dry white wine
4	partridges
4 slices	bacon
2	Yellow Delicious apples

PREPARATION

Chop cabbage into 8 sections. In a large pot, blanch cabbage in salted boiling water for 5 minutes. Drain and set aside.

In a heavy Dutch-oven, melt salt pork. Add blanched cabbage sections, whole onion studded with a clove, bouquet garni, pepper and white wine. Cover and simmer 1 hour.

PROCEDURE

Preheat oven to 232°C (450°F). Tie partridge legs together. Wrap each partridge with a slice of bacon, and place on a roasting pan. Brown in oven.

Place the partridge in Dutch-oven on stovetop with cabbage. Continue cooking, at moderate heat, for 30 minutes. Peel and core apples, cut into 8 sections and add to the preparation. Cook another 30 minutes. Adjust seasoning and serve.

"In June the partridge,
which is so shy a bird,
led her brood from the woods
to the front of my cabin,
clucking and calling to them like a hen,
and in all her behavior
proving herself the hen of the woods."

Henry David Thoreau

Marinated and Grilled Beef Bavette
with Cranberry Chutney

Serves 4

675 g (1½ lb)	beef bavette
100 ml (½ cup)	vegetable oil
50 ml (¼ cup)	red wine vinegar
1	shallot, finely chopped
1 sprig	fresh thyme
1 sprig	fresh rosemary
5 ml (1 tsp)	ground pepper
3	juniper berries
1 sprig	fresh parsley, chopped
1 clove	garlic, chopped

CHUTNEY

1	onion, chopped
2	apples, diced, with peel
120 g (½ cup)	granulated sugar
120 ml (½ cup)	red wine vinegar
1 pinch	Cayenne pepper
1 pinch	ginger powder
2 g (½ tsp)	pickling spices
2 g (½ tsp)	salt
250 g (1 cup)	fresh cranberries

PREPARATION, 24 HOURS IN ADVANCE
Mix together vegetable oil, vinegar, shallot, thyme, rosemary, pepper, juniper berries, parsley and garlic.
Place beef bavette in a freezer bag. Add marinade and seal. Refrigerate for at least 24 hours.

PREPARATION OF CHUTNEY
Mix together all ingredients, except cranberries.
Bring to a boil, reduce heat and simmer until apples are tender. Add cranberries and continue cooking for a few minutes.

PROCEDURE
Preheat barbecue or grooved cast-iron cooking grill.
Drain and pat dry bavette. Season with salt. Sear bavette on hot grill, turn and complete cooking. Remove and let stand for a few minutes covered with aluminum foil.

PRESENTATION
Cut bavette into thin slices. Serve on a warm plate with cranberry chutney.

GOD GRANT THAT I MAY CATCH A FI[SH]
SO BIG THAT EVEN I
WHEN TALKING OF IT AFTERWARDS
MAY NEVER NEED TO LIE

Veal Medallions
Roquefort Sauce

Serves 4

600 g (1 1/3 lb)	veal *or* venison loin
100 g (1/3 cup)	flour
60 ml (1/4 cup)	vegetable oil

ROQUEFORT SAUCE

1	shallot, chopped
125 ml (1/2 cup)	dry white wine
500 ml (2 cups)	brown veal stock
125 ml (1/2 cup)	whipping cream
50 g (2 oz)	Roquefort cheese

PREPARATION

Debone and cut veal loin into 1.5 cm (1/2 in) medallions. Tap meat gently with a mallet. Salt, pepper and flour medallions.

PROCEDURE

In a frying pan, heat vegetable oil. When hot, sear medallions for a few minutes on each side. Set medallions aside and keep warm. Remove excess fat from frying pan.

PREPARATION OF THE SAUCE

In the saucepan, add white wine and chopped shallot. Reduce by half. Add veal stock and reduce again until sauce coats the back of a spoon. Add cream and cheese. Reduce for another 2 minutes. Adjust seasoning.

PRESENTATION

Serve medallions in hot plates with Roquefort sauce.

Pork Mignons
with Pears and Maple Syrup

Serves 4

2	pears
30 ml (2 Tbsp)	butter
2	pork fillets
45 ml (3 Tbsp)	vegetable oil
15 ml (1 Tbsp)	shallot, chopped
45 ml (3 Tbsp)	maple syrup
45 ml (3 Tbsp)	white wine vinegar
400 ml (1²/₃ cups)	brown veal stock
60 ml (¹/₄ cup)	whipping cream

PREPARATION
Peel pears, cut in 6 sections and remove core. With a small paring knife, carefully round each pear section. Keep peel and core for the sauce. In a frying pan, melt butter, add pear sections to colour for a few minutes. Season with salt and pepper. Set aside and keep warm.

PROCEDURE
Preheat oven to 160°C (325°F).
Trim pork fillets. Season with salt and pepper.
In a frying pan, heat oil and sear pork about 2 minutes on each side. Place frying pan in oven for 7 to 8 minutes, depending on the size of the fillets. Remove pork from frying pan and keep warm.

Remove excess fat from frying pan, add chopped shallot, the peel and core of the pear, maple syrup and white wine vinegar. Cook for 1 minute. Add veal stock or a commercial demi-glace and add more water than specified. Simmer for about 5 minutes. In a blender, purée sauce and pass through a sieve. Add cream and cook for a few more minutes until sauce coats the back of a spoon.

FINAL PREPARATION AND PRESENTATION
Cut pork into slices. Pour pear sauce on bottom of a warm plate and fan out pork mignons. Garnish with 3 sautéed pear sections, accompanied with a serving of vegetables and potatoes.

"There was a strange, other-world
remoteness about this place, an atmosphere
peaceful yet definable of presence,
...almost obscured by bracken,
of a croft, and suddenly feeling
that all around me was a listening,
awaiting expectancy."

Sheila Burnford

Beef Fillet in Pastry
with a Hint of Hidden Goat Cheese

Serves 4

4	beef *or* game fillets, 3 cm (1¹/₄ in) thick
45 ml (3 Tbsp)	vegetable oil
60 g (¹/₄ cup)	melted, clarified butter
4 sheets	phyllo pastry
200 g (7 oz)	goat cheese paillot

SAUCE
45 ml (3 Tbsp)	shallot, finely chopped
150 ml (²/₃ cup)	dry red wine
300 ml (1¹/₃ cups)	demi-glace

PREPARATION

Season beef fillets with salt and pepper. In a frying pan, heat oil and rapidly sear meat. Remove from heat and refrigerate.

Melt butter over low heat without colouring. Clarify by removing foam that forms on top and buttermilk deposit at bottom.

PROCEDURE

Preheat oven to 205°C (400°F).

Brush a sheet of phyllo pastry with clarified butter and fold in two. Place a beef fillet on pastry and cover with a slice of goat cheese. Fold pastry and wrap tightly. Place on a cooking sheet. Bake for about 15 minutes or until phyllo is golden brown.

PREPARATION OF THE SAUCE

In a small saucepan, add shallot and red wine. Bring to a boil, and reduce by half. Add demi-glace and reduce until sauce coats the back of a spoon. Pour through a sieve and adjust seasoning.

"...such is autumn on the south slope of the mountain,
    where red oak, yellow birch and orange maples billow in the wind,
    you will see, it is symphonic, and truly Mozart."

Robert Lalonde

Quail and Lentil
Soup

Serves 8

QUAIL OR PARTRIDGE STOCK

1	onion
1	leek
1	carrot
2 stalks	celery
4	quails
1 kg (2 lb)	quail *or* partridge bones
1 ml (¹/₄ tsp)	peppercorns
1 sprig	thyme
1	onion
1 stalk	celery
2	carrots
30 ml (2 Tbsp)	butter
375 g (2 cups)	green lentils
2¹/₄ L (10 cups)	quail *or* other poultry stock
1	bouquet garni

PREPARATION OF THE STOCK
In a large stockpot, cover onion, leek, carrot, celery stalks, quails and bones with cold water. Add peppercorns and thyme. Bring to a boil. Skim and simmer. When quails are almost done, remove the quail's breasts and set aside. Continue simmering for 1 hour 45 minutes. Pour stock through chinois or sieve.

PROCEDURE
Chop onion, celery and carrots. In a saucepan, melt butter. Sweat the vegetables. Add quail stock and lentils. Bring to a boil, add bouquet garni. Simmer for one hour or until lentils are tender. Remove bouquet garni.
In a blender, purée soup and pass through a chinois or a sieve. Season with salt and pepper. Add stock if needed to adjust consistency.

PRESENTATION
Serve soup in warm bowls and add half a quail's breast in each bowl. The breast can be cut in thin slices.

"That night I felt the winter in my veins,
A joyous tremor of the icy glow;
And woke to hear the north's wild vibrant strains
while far and wide, by withered woods and plains,
Fast fell the driving snow."

Wilfred Campbell

"The Flight of the Geese"

Two Pepper Guinea Fowl

Serves 2

2	suprêmes of Guinea fowl *or* partridge
45 ml (3 Tbsp)	olive oil
To garnish	bell peppers of various colours

BELL PEPPER STUFFING

	Meat from legs and fillets of Guinea fowl *or* partridge
1/4	red bell pepper, chopped
1/4	yellow bell pepper, chopped
2	shallots, chopped

SAUCE

2	shallots, finely chopped
30 ml (2 Tbsp)	olive oil
30 ml (2 Tbsp)	red wine vinegar
60 ml (1/4 cup)	dry red wine
180 ml (3/4 cup)	brown chicken stock
1 sprig	rosemary, finely chopped
125 ml (1/2 cup)	whipping cream

PREPARATION OF STUFFING
With a meat grinder, grind all the stuffing ingredients. Season with salt and pepper.

PROCEDURE
Insert tip of sharp knife in the suprêmes. Without piercing, lift to form a cavity. Place stuffing in a pastry bag and fill suprême cavities. Skin will stretch. Preheat oven to 180°C (350°F).
Season suprêmes with salt and pepper. In a frying pan, heat olive oil and sear suprêmes. Cook in oven for 25 minutes. Remove and cover with aluminum foil.

PREPARATION OF THE SAUCE
In a saucepan, sweat shallots in olive oil until soft. Deglaze with red wine vinegar. Add brown chicken stock and red wine. Reduce by half. Add rosemary and cream. Reduce again until sauce coats the back of a spoon. Season with salt and pepper.

FINAL PREPARATION AND PRESENTATION
In the frying pan used for suprêmes, sauté bell pepper strips. Slice suprêmes and serve on warm plate with the sauce and accompanied with mashed sweet potatoes and sautéed bell peppers.

Recipe by Guy Ernst

"High through the drenched and hollow night their wings
beat northward hard on winter's trail. The sound
Of their confused and solemn voices, borne

Athwart the dark to their long Artic morn,
Comes with a sanction and an awe profound,
A boding of unknown, foreshadowed things."

Sir Charles G.D. Roberts

Goose Confit with Salad

Serves 4

GOOSE CONFIT

4	goose legs
60ml (¹/₄ cup)	unrefined coarse salt
60ml (¹/₄ cup)	granulated sugar
1 section	apple
125 ml (¹/₂ cup)	goose fat
125 ml (¹/₂ cup)	olive oil

SALAD

1 L (4 cups)	salad greens
30 ml (2 Tbsp)	shallot, chopped
45ml (3 Tbsp)	olive oil
30ml (2 Tbsp)	white wine vinegar

PROCEDURE, A FEW HOURS IN ADVANCE

In a tightly-sealed container, cover goose legs with salt and sugar. Refrigerate 2 hours.
Preheat oven to 135°C (275°F).
Rinse legs and pat dry. In a saucepan, cover legs and apple section with goose fat and olive oil. Cook in oven for 3 hours or until tender. Cool. Debone and cover meat completely with cooking fat. Refrigerate.

FINAL PREPARATION AND PRESENTATION

Sweat shallot in 15 ml (1 Tbsp) olive oil. Deglaze with wine vinegar and add remaining olive oil. Season with salt and pepper to taste. Pour on salad with some warm goose confit.

Lamb Crépinette with Salted Herbs

Serves 2

150 g (1/3 lb)	pig's caul
200 g (1/2 lb)	ground lamb *or* pork
200 ml (3/4 cup)	whipping cream
15 ml (1 Tbsp)	salted herbs
15 ml (1 Tbsp)	shallot, chopped
60 ml (1/4 cup)	fresh parsley, chopped
1	lamb loin, boneless and trimmed
30 ml (2 Tbsp)	vegetable oil

SALTED HERB SAUCE

500 ml (2 cups)	lamb stock
15 ml (1 Tbsp)	salted herbs
30 ml (2 Tbsp)	butter
30 ml (2 Tbsp)	flour
15 ml (1 Tbsp)	butter

PREPARATION OF STUFFING

In a food processor, finely chop lamb or pork meat. Add cream while blending. Place in a bowl, add salted herbs, shallot and 15 ml (1 Tbsp) parsley. Season with salt and pepper.

PREPARATION OF THE SAUCE

In a saucepan, pour lamb stock. Add salted herbs, and bring to a boil. Meanwhile, mix 30 ml (2 Tbsp) butter with flour. After five minutes, add flour and butter mixture to lamb stock, whisking constantly. Continue to cook for 10 minutes. When sauce is ready, add remaining butter and keep whisking. Correct seasoning and keep warm.

PROCEDURE

Preheat oven to 150°C (300°F). Drain off and pat dry pig's caul, spread on a work surface. Sprinkle with 3 spoonfuls chopped parsley on the caul, spread stuffing evenly to cover caul almost completely. Place lamb loin in the middle and tightly roll up caul so that stuffing completely surrounds loin.

FIFTEEN MINUTES BEFORE SERVING

In a frying pan, heat vegetable oil. When hot, sear crépinette on all sides. Place in oven for 10 minutes. Remove, cover with aluminum foil and let stand 5 minutes before serving.

FINAL PREPARATION AND PRESENTATION

Cut crépinette into thick slices. Place in a warm plate, and serve with salted herb sauce.

Pigeons in Clay

Serves 4

125 g (1/4 lb)	salt pork
16	white pearl onions
100 g (1 cup)	mushrooms
15 ml (1 Tbsp)	olive oil
4	pigeons
100 g (1/4 lb)	pork bard
1 sprig	fresh thyme

PREPARATION

Soak clay pot for 20 minutes in cold water. Cut salt pork, peel small onions and cut mushrooms in quarters.

PROCEDURE

Preheat oven to 200°C (400°F).

In a frying pan, sear salt pork in hot oil. Add pearl onions and mushrooms. Brown lightly. Place in bottom of clay pot. Tie legs and cover breasts with a thin layer of pork bard. Pepper to taste. Place pigeons in clay pot over salt pork and vegetables. Add thyme. Cover and bake in oven for about 30 minutes, depending on size of pigeons. Adjust seasoning.

PRESENTATION

Remove string and pork bard. Serve with cooking juices.

"But the woods were gorgeous with colour, and the swamps a scarlet maze of cranberry bushes.
The sky was infinitely remote and blue, with scarcely a cloud sailing."

Martha Ostenso

Whitetailed Deer Osso Buco

Serves 6

1	onion, chopped
2 stalks	celery, chopped
2 cloves	garlic, chopped
3	tomatoes
25 ml (1^1/$_2$ Tbsp)	olive oil
25 g (1^1/$_2$ Tbsp)	butter
100 ml (1/4 cup)	flour
1.5 kg (3 lb)	deer shanks
45 ml (3 Tbsp)	olive oil
1	bay leaf
1 sprig	fresh thyme
250 ml (1 cup)	dry white wine
1 L (4 cups)	beef stock
30 ml (2 Tbsp)	fresh parsley, chopped
1/4	lemon zest, finely grated

BEEF STOCK
1 kg (2.2 lb)	beef bones
3	carrots, chopped
1	onion, chopped
2 cloves	garlic
1	bay leaf
1	bouquet garni
1 sprig	fresh tarragon

PREPARATION OF BEEF STOCK
Preheat oven to 250°C (480°F). Roast beef bones until well browned.
Place in a stockpot with vegetables, garlic and herbs. Cover with water. Simmer for 2 hours. Skim. Pass through a chinois or a sieve. Refrigerate and remove fat.

PREPARATION
Remove peduncle from tomatoes. Make an incision in the shape of an "x" on top and immerse in boiling water for 10 seconds, then in cold water. Remove skin, cut tomatoes in two and press to remove seeds. Dice. Set aside.

PROCEDURE
Preheat oven to 180°C (350°F).
In a saucepan, heat oil and butter. Sweat onions and celery. Flour deer shanks, using all the flour. Season with salt and pepper.
In a frying pan, heat oil. Sear shanks on each side. Transfer to saucepan, add garlic, bay leaf, thyme, white wine, tomatoes and stock. Adjust seasoning. Bring to a boil, cover and place in oven for an hour and a half, or until meat is tender. Remove thyme and bay leaf.

FINAL PREPARATION AND PRESENTATION
Mix parsley and lemon zest.
Place deer shanks on a warm serving platter, coat with sauce and sprinkle with parsley and lemon zest mixture. Serve with pasta.

"What moves Hector, what he hears in the forest of his heart, is this cry,
    this call of the feverish beast; this voice intermingled with the perfume of autumn;
of passion and of night resonating within his flesh like a horn."

Félix-Antoine Savard

Caribou, Wild Boar and Pheasant
Pot-au-feu

Serves 8

8	young carrots
8	young turnips
2 stalks	celery
1	small Savoy cabbage
8	young potatoes
8	small leeks
2	corn-cobs
250 g (¹/₂ lb)	green beans
3 L (12 cups)	beef stock
10	peppercorns
15 ml (1 Tbsp)	coarse salt
1	bouquet garni (bay leaf, thyme, parsley)
1	onion, studded with two whole cloves
450 g (1 lb)	salted boar flank *or* lean salt pork
700 g (1¹/₂ lb)	caribou *or* moose, cut into large cubes
4	pheasant suprêmes (breasts)
120 ml (¹/₂ cup)	white wine vinegar
60 ml (¹/₄ cup)	coarse salt

PREPARATION
Peel carrots and turnips, keeping a bit of the stem. Cut celery into 10 cm (4 in) pieces, and cabbage into 8 sections. Wash potatoes, remove roots from leeks and wash, peel corn-cobs and cut into 6 cm (2 in) sections, tie green beans into small bundles. Set aside.

PROCEDURE
In a large stockpot, combine beef stock, peppercorns, coarse salt to taste, bouquet garni and onion. Bring to a boil, simmer for 10 minutes.
Add salted boar or salt pork, cook for 15 minutes. Add caribou cubes and continue simmering for 30 minutes. Add pheasant breasts and simmer for another 30 minutes. Add carrots, turnips, celery, cabbage and cook for 15 minutes. Add potatoes, leeks and corn and cook for 15 minutes. Add green beans and continue cooking for another 15 minutes. Remove from heat.

FINAL PREPARATION AND PRESENTATION
Place meat and vegetables on a large, warm serving platter. Serve with cooking juices, vinegar and coarse salt.

Moose Fillet
with Cloudberry* Sauce

Serves 4

700 g (1¹/₂ lb)	moose *or* beef fillet
45 ml (3 Tbsp)	vegetable oil

CLOUDBERRY OR GOOSEBERRY SAUCE

45 ml (3 Tbsp)	Chicoutai liqueur
60 ml (¹/₄ cup)	shallot, chopped
125 ml (¹/₂ cup)	Dégel d'amour® mead honey wine (made with cloudberries) *or* dry white wine
250 ml (1 cup)	game *or* veal demi-glace
60 ml (4 Tbsp)	cloudberry *or* gooseberry jam

PROCEDURE
Preheat oven to 150°C (300°F).
Tie moose or beef fillet with kitchen string, season with salt and pepper. In a frying pan, heat oil and sear fillet on all sides. Once well browned, place in oven for about 10 minutes, depending on desired doneness. Remove fillet from oven, cover with aluminum foil. Keep warm and let stand for 5 minutes. Keep pan drippings for sauce.

PREPARATION OF CLOUDBERRY SAUCE
Skim fat from drippings and deglaze with Chicoutai liqueur. Add shallot and mead honey wine. Bring to a boil and reduce until almost dry. Add demi-glace, bring to a boil and simmer 5 minutes. Pass through a sieve. Add cloudberry jam. Heat and season to taste.

FINAL PREPARATION AND PRESENTATION
Remove string from fillet and cut into thick slices. Place meat on warm plates and serve with the sauce.

* *Cloudberry or chicoutai: small berry, at first red, then amber and translucent, it resembles a raspberry and is found in the North and around the Gulf of Saint Lawrence.*

Deer
Liver Roast

Serves 8

1	deer liver (*or* another large game animal)
2 ml (¹/₂ tsp)	four-spice
75 ml (¹/₃ cup)	Cognac
1	shallot, chopped
400 ml (1³/₄ cups)	demi-glace (*or* 1 package powdered demi-glace)
50 g (3 Tbsp)	butter

PROCEDURE

Preheat oven to 220°C (425°F).

With kitchen string, tie deer liver in the shape of a roast. Place in a roasting pan. Season with salt, pepper, four-spice and 30 ml (2 Tbsp) Cognac. Place in oven and cook for 10 minutes.

Reduce temperature to 160°C (325°F) and continue cooking for 15 minutes. Remove roast, place on warm platter and cover with aluminum foil.

Deglaze pan with remaining Cognac, and flambée. Add shallot and demi-glace (for powdered demi-glace, add 400 ml (1³/₄ cups) water). Reduce sauce for a few minutes. Pass through a chinois or a sieve, pouring into a small saucepan.

Bring to a boil and add butter while whipping.

FINAL PREPARATION AND PRESENTATION

Remove string from roast, slice and serve on a warm plate with the sauce.

Aldée and the king of the forest

A story told by Dave Boulet

Autumn officially arrives in Quebec when the maples turn red and the first frost tinges the rocky soil of the Appalachians. And autumn's arrival signals the approaching moose hunt. Only a handful of seasoned guides know the Quebec forest and this majestic animal well enough to virtually assure their sports a successful hunt.

This story, told by Dave Boulet, chronicles just one of the adventures of the legendary moose-hunting guide, Aldée Beaumont. Hailing from Stoneham, north of Quebec City, Aldée's chiseled features and deeply-lined face bespeak a life spent outdoors, a life dedicated to the understanding and conservation of the Laurentian fauna. For 35 years he worked for the Department of Wildlife and Natural Resources, 30 of those studying moose in the field. His knowledge of the wild is impressive and his resume includes helping reintroduce caribou into the Parc des Grands Jardins, in the heart of the Charlevoix World Biosphere Reserve.

"We were having a hell of a season that fall at Lake Portage. Two of our three clients had downed a moose: the first on the Sunday and the second one Monday, both in the Dead Waters territory. Both animals were males, one with an antler rack that measured 35 inches. The third client, an American from Detroit, had already missed a couple of good shots. Aldée was his guide.

Aldée doesn't speak English, but he speaks "moose". He understands *moose, shoot, track, truck, good morning, yes, no and toaster*. He walks alongside his client through the region's rugged terrain; through the branches and over the rocks.

Photo : Aldée Beaumont

Nor does this seasoned woodsman believe much in modern hunting practices. For example, while we dress in camouflage, he hunts with his red and black checkered vest. While we use odors like mare's urine to cover our scent, Aldée smokes... We leave for the hunt half an hour before the crack of dawn; he leaves half an hour after sunrise because he doesn't want his clients to wander away in the woods. We hunt in the morning and in the evening; he kills just as many at noon. We are taught by the "experts" on their cassettes to utter small, soft calls; when Aldée calls, the mountains shake. He believes in challenging, not seducing. When he starts off with his loud calls, he says, "on va aller les chercher au Maine!" [we'll go get them in Maine]

Off for a morning hunt, Aldée leaves with his little toque rolled up on his head, his cigarette, his red and black checked vest, and his binoculars hung around his neck with binder twine. He looks like the Quebec hunter of 20 or 30 years ago, like the guide you expect when you think of Quebec.

Getting back to my story, Aldée's bow-hunter client had already missed two golden chances, and now there were no more moose in sight – not even any tracks. So, Aldée suggested returning to the Dead Waters, the lucky sector. The other guides and hunters thought perhaps the master was losing it; they didn't believe there could be a third animal in that territory.

But back they go and Aldée calls. A moose answers. By the resonance of the voice, he knows it is a large male.

The rutting animal approaches. But he was already courting a nearby female who now calls him back. Again Aldée calls the male, imitating a love-struck female. But the real one calls again. It's a competition. The bull can't make up its mind and refuses to come out of the forest.

After several hours, deciding to go for broke, Aldée changes his tune, and snorts out a big bull's call. If the moose won't come for love, perhaps it will for a fight. This tactic could backfire because if it's a small male, and you imitate a big bull by breaking branches and trees, the target might beat a retreat, judging that his adversary is too dominant. But if it's a big one, you expect him to see red and break through trees. That's what big bulls do when they make up their mind during the rut: neither trees nor branches can resist their passage. The animal has poor eyesight, and so compensates with an exceptional strength, a keen sense of smell and a well-developed sense of hearing.

Three hours after the first call, Aldée gambles. He breaks down trees with trunks that measure 20 centimetres. Crack, crack; the sound of snapping trees carries through the forest. Now the moose, thinking he has to contend with an adversary, comes forward. He smashes trees and breaks branches creating an extraordinary uproar. The two hunters are crouching on the ground – no observation towers in this territory.

Expecting the moose to use the trail, Aldée puts the hunter beside the trail, between the approaching beast and himself. He stays well away to force the moose to pass in front of the hunter. The moose approaches, not going around trees but through them. He is knocking everything down like a clear-cutter. The hunter, crouching down along the trail, sees the moose emerge. After three hours of "playing games" with Aldée, it's furious and wants at its rival.

And who does the moose see? Aldée. Its ears turn down, the hairs along his back bristle. This is not a happy moose. While rare, even after "recognizing" Aldée, the moose moves toward him. The beast is immense.

Imagine the scene. Aldée backs up and finds himself at the foot of a rocky spur and a small mountain. He squeezes back further shouting, "shoot, Shoot! SHOOT!!!" The moose is directly in front of the hunter, who now, to make things worse, is suffering from buck fever. There, 18 feet away, is a monster with a 52-inch rack, and he has to hit it with an arrow. Aldée backs a little ways up the spur. The moose only has eyes – nasty red ones – for him. It's a dominant male, the king of the forest, and Aldée knows he's in trouble if his "frozen" client doesn't soon let fly. Once again he yells at the bowman to shoot, opening his vest to show the orange inside, hoping to spook the animal. It isn't looking good, Aldée has no gun, his client still hasn't reacted, and the moose is ready to charge. Finally, the client looses a shaft. The beast circles round twice and collapses. It turned out to be one of the largest animals ever brought down in the territory.

Ice fishing

...What a white-out! It must be minus 40 on the ice.
...My camera no longer works, frozen solid! Quickly, I have to reheat it for several minutes inside my parka.

...Jean-Paul had warned us this morning at breakfast... "My friends, we're going to have to dress warmly," he said. "I'm just back from lighting the stove in the cabin... I'm used to the cold, but this morning we're breaking records. The wind burns our face!"

"...You, Ma'am, you're going to freeze solid in that little fur coat! We've got a spare snowmobile suit and Réjeanne will let you use it. And you Mr. Photographer, you'll have to put on several sweaters under your parka..."

That advice was much appreciated later as I sat on the pile of firewood in a sleigh pulled behind the snowmobile! In spite of the cold we cannot help but be impressed by the immensity and the beauty of the landscape. Occasionally the rays of the sun pierce the blowing snow, adding to the eeriness of the place, and giving a golden tint to the hard-packed snow on the ice.

...How can one do justice to such a fantastic landscape with a simple camera?

...But now my friends are busy around the fishing lines! ...I am sure these activities will deliver a good hot fish soup for supper.

Paul-E. Lambert

The Photographer's Fish Soup

Serves 8

30 ml (2 Tbsp)	olive oil
125 ml (1/2 cup)	carrot, diced
50 ml (1/4 cup)	celery, diced
50 ml (1/4 cup)	shallot, chopped
2.5 ml (1/2 tsp)	curry powder
1 pinch	Cayenne pepper
1 pinch	savory
1.5 L (6 cups)	chicken stock
250 ml (1 cup)	potatoes, diced
125 ml (1/2 cup)	corn kernels
125 ml (1/2 cup)	milk
50 ml (1/4 cup)	flour
30 ml (2 Tbsp)	green onion, chopped
15 ml (1 Tbsp)	fresh Italian parsley, chopped
450 g (1 lb)	fish (red fish *or* any white fish)

PROCEDURE

In a large pot, heat olive oil and sweat carrot, celery and shallot. Add curry powder, Cayenne pepper and savory. Pour in chicken stock, add potatoes, corn kernels and bring to a boil. Whisk flour into cold milk, and add to soup, stirring well. Add green onion. Simmer soup for 10 minutes. Add fish, cut into large cubes, season with salt and pepper and simmer for a few more minutes. Add parsley.

PRESENTATION

Serve soup in hot bowls with sourdough bread.

Tarragon Granita

Serves 8

450 ml (2 cups)	water
115 g (1/2 cup)	granulated sugar
60 ml (1/4 cup)	fresh tarragon leaves
1/4	lemon
8 sprigs	fresh tarragon

PROCEDURE, A FEW HOURS IN ADVANCE

In a saucepan, mix water and sugar and bring to a boil. Place tarragon leaves in a mixing bowl. As soon as syrup begins boiling, pour onto tarragon leaves and add lemon juice. Remove from heat and infuse for 20 minutes. Pour syrup through a chinois or a sieve into a rectangular metal container. Place in freezer for about 3 hours. Every hour, stir with a fork until granita becomes granulated. Granita can also be made more quickly with an ice cream maker.

FINAL PREPARATION AND PRESENTATION

Place goblets in freezer for an hour.
Move granita from freezer to refrigerator before serving.
Serve in iced goblets. Garnish with tarragon sprigs.

Pepper Ice Cream

Serves 8

500 ml (2 cups)	milk
250 ml (1 cup)	whipping cream
10 g (1 Tbsp)	black peppercorns, roughly crushed
6	egg yolks
240 g (1 cup)	granulated sugar

PREPARATION, 24 HOURS IN ADVANCE

Place ice cream maker container in freezer.
In a thick bottom saucepan, mix milk, whipping cream and crushed peppercorns. Bring to a boil, remove from heat and infuse for 10 minutes. Pass through a fine sieve.
Beat egg yolks and sugar. Pour milk mixture onto beaten egg yolks. Return mixture to saucepan and cook gently until thickened, to 85°C (185°F). Remove immediately from heat, and pour into a bowl through a fine sieve. Stir to cool. Refrigerate 24 hours, to improve taste and consistency.

PROCEDURE

Pour mixture into the frozen ice cream maker container. Churn until ice cream has set. Place in a container in the freezer.

PRESENTATION

Put goblets in freezer for an hour.
Place pepper ice cream in refrigerator 15 minutes before serving.
Serve in iced goblets.

Balsam Fir Jelly Granita

Serves 10

250 ml (1 cup)	balsam fir jelly[1]
575 ml (2 1/2 cups)	water
1/2	lemon

FROSTED FIR BRANCHES

10	small balsam fir branches
1	egg white, beaten
30 ml (2 Tbsp)	granulated sugar

PROCEDURE, A FEW HOURS IN ADVANCE

Bring water to a boil, pour over balsam fir jelly and stir until dissolved. Add juice from half a lemon. Pour mixture into a rectangular metal container. Place in freezer for about 3 hours. Stir every hour with a fork until granita has a granulated consistency. Granita can also be made more quickly with an ice cream maker.

PREPARATION OF FIR BRANCHES

Dip branches into beaten egg white and sprinkle with sugar. Place in freezer until ready to serve.

FINAL PREPARATION AND PRESENTATION

Place goblets in freezer for an hour.
Move granita from freezer to refrigerator before serving.
Using a small ice cream scoop, place granita into goblets. Decorate with frosted fir branch.
Granita should be served before main course, as is a "trou normand."

[1] Balsam fir jelly can be found in gourmet shops or at butcher shops. It goes well with game paté.

"In the album he holds in his thin hands
are the thousand photographs he has made of winter
Each one is perfectly exposed, each one a pure
white with sometimes only the barest of shadows;
a fleeting, ephemeral grey that betrays
the image of who or what it was he took.
It pleases him to go through it slowly and remember"

Patrick Lane

"...Out on de reever de nort' win' blow,
Down on de valley is pile de snow,
But w'at do we care so long we know
We'safe on de log cabane?"

William Henry Drummond

"Grey, unnerved, brown and savage land
you crack in the cold's
ghostly beauty, in tides of birch trees
brotherhoods of spruce, fir and their fellows
among strange rocks   and opposing forces."

Gaston Miron

Vanilla Sherbet
with Spiced Tuiles

Serves 6 (3 dozen small tuiles)

TUILES
125 g (¹/₂ cup)	granulated sugar
75 g (¹/₃ cup + 2 Tbsp)	flour
1	egg
¹/₂	lemon zest, finely grated
2	egg whites
6 ml (1¹/₄ tsp)	five-spice
500 ml (2 cups)	water
125 g (¹/₂ cup)	granulated sugar
1	vanilla bean
¹/₂	lemon, juice
1	egg white

PREPARATION OF TUILES, 24 HOURS IN ADVANCE
Mix together sugar, flour, egg and lemon zest. Add egg whites, five-spice and mix. Refrigerate 24 hours.
Preheat oven to 205°C (400°F).
On a well-buttered cookie sheet, pour mixture, one small spoonful at a time. Flatten tuiles into very thin shapes and bake for about 4 minutes. Tuiles are ready when sides are golden. Remove from cookie sheet and immediately mould tuiles on a rolling pin.

PROCEDURE
Mix water and sugar. Bring to a boil. Remove from heat. Slice the vanilla bean lengthwise and grate it. Add to sugar-water mixture and infuse for 30 minutes. Refrigerate to cool. Add lemon juice and pass through a sieve. Prepare ice cream maker according to manufacturer's instructions. Add ingredients and churn until desired consistency. A few minutes before churning is complete, add egg white. Keep container in freezer.

PRESENTATION ONE HOUR BEFORE SERVING
Place goblets in freezer. Move sherbet from freezer to refrigerator.
Place a few scoops of sherbet into goblets and serve with spiced tuiles.

Apple Phyllo Aumônière
with Cinnamon

Serves 4

CRÈME ANGLAISE
250 ml (1 cup)	milk
2 ml (¹/₄ tsp)	cinnamon
50 g (¹/₄ cup)	granulated sugar
3	egg yolks

CUSTARD
60 g (¹/₄ cup)	granulated sugar
10 g (1 Tbsp)	flour
10 g (1 Tbsp)	cornstarch
2	eggs
250 ml (1 cup)	milk
1.5 ml (¹/₄ tsp)	cinnamon

3	apples
50 g (3 Tbsp)	butter
50 g (¹/₄ cup)	granulated sugar
30 ml (2 Tbsp)	Calvados
4 sheets	phyllo pastry
60 g (¹/₄ cup)	butter

PREPARATION OF CRÈME ANGLAISE, 24 HOURS IN ADVANCE
In a saucepan, heat milk and cinnamon.
Whisk egg yolks and sugar vigorously. While still whisking, pour hot milk into sugar and egg yolk mixture. Pour back into saucepan and heat gently until it reaches 85°C (185°F). Do not boil. Crème anglaise is ready when it coats the back of a spoon. Through a strainer, pour mixture into a bowl. Stir constantly to cool quickly. Refrigerate.

PREPARATION OF CUSTARD
In a mixing bowl, whisk sugar, flour, cornstarch and eggs. In a thick bottom saucepan add milk and cinnamon, bring to a boil. Whisking constantly, add hot milk to sugar and egg mixture. Pour back into saucepan, and bring to a boil, stirring constantly so mixture doesn't stick. Boil for 4 to 5 minutes. Pour custard back into bowl and stir to cool rapidly and to keep smooth. Refrigerate.

PREPARATION OF APPLES
Peel apples, remove core and dice. In a frying pan, melt butter, add apples and sugar. Sauté gently for a few minutes until apples are tender. Add Calvados and flambée. Cool.

PROCEDURE
Melt butter, skim foam, carefully pour butter off milk solids settled at bottom, keeping only clarified butter. Preheat oven to 190°C (375°F).
Cut phyllo pastry sheets in two and brush with clarified butter. Lay one sheet of pastry over another, add two spoonfuls of apple and two spoonfuls of custard. Close, forming the shape of a small purse (aumônière). Bake for about 10 minutes, or until golden brown.

FINAL PREPARATION AND PRESENTATION
Coat bottom of plate with crème anglaise. Place a hot apple phyllo aumônière on plate. Garnish with a cinnamon stick and a few fresh raspberries.

Blueberry and Cinnamon
Parfait

Serves 8

8 sheets	gelatin *or*
14 g (2 packages)	powdered gelatin
1.5 L (2 pints)	blueberries
125 g (¹/₂ cup)	granulated sugar
15 ml (1 Tbsp)	ground cinnamon
75 ml (¹/₃ cup)	Drambuie®
250 ml (1 cup)	whipping cream
30 ml (2 Tbsp)	icing sugar
250 g (8 oz)	cream cheese

PROCEDURE, 5 HOURS IN ADVANCE
Dissolve gelatin according to instructions on package.
In a small saucepan, over low heat, cook blueberries, sugar, Drambuie, cinnamon and the dissolved gelatin 5 to 10 minutes. Cool.
Whip cream with icing sugar and refrigerate. With a mixer, beat cream cheese until smooth. Carefully fold in blueberries and whipped cream mixture into cream cheese. Pour into molds and refrigerate for at least 4 hours.

FINAL PREPARATION AND PRESENTATION
Remove parfait by pouring warm water on the mold. Garnish with blueberries, a cinnamon stick and spices to taste.

Recipe by Véronique Gosselin

"He watched the faraway delicate purple penetrate the forest and give it life. Over the snow, now tinted ever so little with blue, trembled the delicate shadows of young branches. It had been so long since he had seen the exquisite play in which revel the most ordinary things when there is honest light... There was in this water of the heavens, a color to which might properly be ascribed no name known to man..."

Gabrielle Roy

Sugar Pie

SWEET PASTRY FOR TWO PIE CRUSTS

280 g (1¹/₃ cups)	unsalted butter, cold
380 g (2¹/₂ cups)	flour
130 g (¹/₂ cup)	icing sugar
1	egg, beaten
25 ml (5 tsp)	water
5 ml (1 tsp)	vanilla extract

¹/₂ recipe	sweet pastry
60 g (¹/₄ cup)	butter
60 g (¹/₂ cup)	flour
340 g (1¹/₂ cups)	maple sugar *or* brown sugar
125 ml (¹/₂ cup)	whipping cream

PREPARATION OF THE SWEET PASTRY PIE CRUST
Cut cold butter into small cubes. Sift together flour and icing sugar. Cut butter into flour with a pastry cutter. When mixture becomes coarse, add beaten egg, water and vanilla extract. Do not knead the dough too much. Refrigerate for a few hours before rolling out.

PROCEDURE
Preheat oven to 150°C (300°F).
Sprinkle flour on work surface and roll out dough using a flour-coated rolling pin. Place the dough in a 25 cm (10 in) pie mould with a removable bottom.
Mix together butter, flour and sugar. Add whipping cream and mix thoroughly without beating. Pour mixture into the pie crust. Bake on lowest rack of the oven for about 30 to 45 minutes or until pie crust is golden and the filling is firm.
Cool and remove from mould.

Iced Beer Sabayon
La Fin du Monde®

Serves 4

TUILES

1	egg
2	egg whites
125 g (1/2 cup)	granulated sugar
65 g (1/3 cup)	flour
5 ml (1 tsp)	lemon zest
4	egg yolks
150 g (2/3 cup)	granulated sugar
150 ml (5 oz)	La Fin du Monde® beer
250 ml (1 cup)	whipping cream

PROCEDURE FOR TUILES, 12 HOURS IN ADVANCE
Mix together egg, egg whites and sugar. Add flour and lemon zest. Mix well. Refrigerate the dough for 12 hours. Cut out an original shape in heavy cardboard and discard it, keeping the cut cardboard.
Preheat oven to 180°C (350°F).
Butter a pastry sheet. Place the cardboard shape on the pastry sheet. Spread some of the tuile mixture within the shape. Use a spatula to make a thin, even layer of pastry. The cardboard cut out must be very flat on the sheet.
Bake for 8 to 12 minutes. As soon as the tuile is taken out of the oven, place it onto a bottle to form it. A tip: Bake the tuiles one at a time and keep the dough cold.

PROCEDURE, SEVERAL HOURS IN ADVANCE
In bain-marie, mix the egg yolks, the sugar and the beer. Place on heat and whisk constantly until frothy. The mixture should become thick and smooth, with a good consistency. Remove from heat and stir until it has cooled.
Whip the cream until it forms firm peaks. Fold the first mixture into the whipped cream.
Pour into plastic molds or into goblets. Place in freezer for several hours.

PRESENTATION
Remove the frozen sabayon from the freezer and place in the refrigerator 20 minutes before serving.
Serve the sabayon onto a cold plate, garnish with a tuile and a few fresh berries.

Strawberry and Blackberry
Mousse

Serves 8

STRAWBERRY MOUSSE

1/2 L (1 pint)	fresh strawberries
7 g (1 envelope)	unflavoured gelatin
50 g (1/4 cup)	granulated sugar
200 ml (7/8 cup)	whipping cream

BLACKBERRY MOUSSE
Same quantities as for strawberry mousse

TO DECORATE
Mint leaves

PREPARATION
In a blender, purée strawberries to obtain 175 g (3/4 cup) fruit pulp. Do the same with the blackberries. Keep some berries aside for decoration.

PROCEDURE, A FEW HOURS IN ADVANCE
In a mixing bowl, sprinkle gelatin onto 50 ml (1/4 cup) water, let rest for a minute. Add 50 ml (1/4 cup) boiling water, and stir until gelatin is completely dissolved.

Heat strawberry purée along with sugar. Add dissolved gelatin, stir well. Remove from heat and refrigerate.

Whip cream until soft peaks form. Fold fruit purée mixture into whipped cream. Pour into goblets until half full.

Prepare blackberry mousse in the same way. Pour over strawberry mousse.

PRESENTATION
Garnish each goblet with half a strawberry, a blackberry and a mint leaf.

Lemon Cream
Tarts

Makes 12 tarts

SWEET CRUST PASTRY

140 g (²/₃ cup)	unsalted butter, cold
190 g (1¹/₄ cups)	flour
65 g (¹/₄ cup)	icing sugar
¹/₂	egg, beaten
13 ml (2¹/₂ tsp)	cold water
2 ml (¹/₂ tsp)	vanilla extract
30 g (1 oz)	chocolate

LEMON CREAM

100 ml (7 Tbsp)	fresh lemon juice
200 g (1 cup)	granulated sugar
130 g (¹/₂ cup + 1 Tbsp)	unsalted butter
20 g (2 Tbsp)	cornstarch
4	eggs, whole

**PREPARATION OF SWEET CRUST PASTRY,
A FEW HOURS IN ADVANCE**
Cut butter into small cubes. Sift together flour and icing sugar. With a pastry cutter, cut butter into flour mixture until coarse. Add beaten egg, water and vanilla extract. Mix carefully without overworking dough.
Wrap and refrigerate dough a few hours before rolling.

BAKING TART SHELLS
Preheat oven to 180°C (350°F).
On a work surface, spread flour and roll out dough with rolling pin. Place dough into tart moulds. Refrigerate 30 minutes.
Cut small circles of wax paper the size of the tart moulds. Place wax paper on dough in each mould and fill with dry peas to prevent dough from rising.
Bake until pastry is golden. Cool. Remove dry peas and wax paper.
Melt chocolate and brush on bottom of tart shells.

PREPARATION OF LEMON CREAM
In a bain-marie, mix lemon juice, sugar, unsalted butter and cornstarch. Bring to a boil, stirring constantly.
Beat eggs and while beating constantly, pour lemon mixture onto eggs.
Return to bain-marie and cook, stirring constantly, until mixture thickens.
Pour lemon cream into tart shells. Serve.

Pears Poached
in Red Wine

Serves 6

6	fresh pears
15 ml (1 Tbsp)	lemon juice
375 g (1²/3 cups)	granulated sugar
375 ml (1²/3 cups)	water
375 ml (1²/3 cups)	red wine
1	vanilla bean
6 leaves	mint

PREPARATION, SEVERAL HOURS BEFORE SERVING
Peel and core the pears, leaving stem on each. To keep the pears from browning, sprinkle with lemon juice.
In a large saucepan, mix sugar, water, red wine and vanilla bean split lengthwise and scraped. Bring to a boil. Simmer for 5 minutes. Add pears to red wine syrup. Bring to a boil, and simmer for 15 minutes or until the pears are tender.
Place a plate over the pears to submerge them in the syrup and cool for several hours.

PRESENTATION
Serve the pears chilled along with the syrup. Garnish with a mint leaf.

Tarte Nicol

Serves 8 to 10

1	22 cm (9 in) sweet pastry pie crust
125 ml (1/2 cup)	raspberry jam
3	Yellow Delicious apples

PROCEDURE

Preheat oven to 190°C (375°F).
Spread a little jam on the bottom of the pie crust.
Peel apples, cut in two and remove core. Cut apples into thin slices and fan them out onto the jam.
Bake pie for about 30 minutes on lowest rack of the oven. When cooked, brush remaining warmed raspberry jam onto the pie and heat. Cool before removing from pan.

PRESENTATION

Serve Tarte Nicol with a crème anglaise or a vanilla ice cream.

...A few ingredients, imagination and an inspirational setting. This pie was first prepared at the Club Nicol, on the banks of the Batiscan River.

Plum Pie

Serves 8 to 10

1	22 cm (9 in) sweet pastry pie crust
650 g (1 1/2 lb)	fresh plums
60 g (1/4 cup)	granulated sugar
60 g (1/4 cup)	almonds, slivered

PROCEDURE

Preheat oven to 190°C (375°F).
Pit the plums and split in half. Spread on the bottom of the pie crust. Sprinkle sugar and almonds on the fruit.
Bake pie for about 30 minutes on the lowest rack of the oven. Cool before removing from pie pan.

"Outside the window
is the rain, green
because it is summer, and beyond that
the trees and then the world..."

Margaret Atwood

Seasonal Pies
à la Kristine

FRESH BERRY PIE

Serves 8

BISCUIT PASTRY

125 g (1/2 cup)	butter
200 ml (1 cup)	brown sugar
110 g (3/4 cup)	flour
7 ml (1/2 Tbsp)	poppy seeds
1/8	lemon zest
75 g (3/4 cup)	almond powder
300 g (3 cups)	raspberries
250 g (2 cups)	strawberries
200 g (2 cups)	blueberries
50 ml (1/4 cup)	water
220 ml (1 cup)	granulated sugar
1	vanilla bean, cut lengthwise

PREPARATION OF BISCUIT PASTRY, A FEW HOURS IN ADVANCE

Mix together butter and brown sugar. Add flour, poppy seeds, lemon zest and almond powder.
On a piece of waxed paper, flatten the biscuit mix to about 1 cm (1/3 inch). Cut into desired shape and refrigerate.

PREPARATION OF THE BERRIES

Wash the berries.
Simmer all ingredients with the fruits for 30 to 40 minutes until slightly thickened.
Pour the mixture into a 22 cm (9 in) pie pan.

PROCEDURE

Preheat oven to 180°C (350°F).
Place the biscuit dough over the fruit mixture and bake until crust is golden.

GROUND CHERRIES IN CRUST

Serves 4

BISCUIT PASTRY

60 g (1/4 cup)	butter
100 ml (1/2 cup)	brown sugar
75 g (1/2 cup)	flour
300 g (2 1/4 cups)	ground cherries (physalis)
75 ml (1/3 cup)	water
75 g (1/3 cup)	granulated sugar
15 g (1 Tbsp)	butter
1/2	vanilla bean, cut lengthwise

PREPARATION OF THE BISCUIT PASTRY, A FEW HOURS IN ADVANCE

Mix together butter and brown sugar. Add flour. On a piece of waxed paper, flatten the biscuit mix to about 1 cm (1/3 in). Cut into desired shape and refrigerate.

PREPARATION OF THE FRUIT

Simmer all the ingredients with the fruit for about half an hour to obtain a syrupy consistency. Reduce the liquid if necessary. Pour mixture into a 15 cm (6 in) pie pan.

PROCEDURE

Preheat oven to 180°C (350°F).
Place biscuit dough onto fruit mixture and bake until crust is golden.

Recipes by Kristine Laflamme

"...the blue flag (Iris Versicolor) grows thinly in the pure water, rising from the stony bottom all around the shore... and the color both of its bluish blades and its flowers,

Fresh Fruit Gratin
with Caramelized Hazelnuts

Serves 4

HAZELNUT PRALINE

50 g (1/4 cup)	granulated sugar
15 ml (1 Tbsp)	water
50 g (3/8 cup)	hazelnuts, whole
500 ml (2 cups)	assorted fruit
3	egg yolks
60 g (1/4 cup)	granulated sugar
85 ml (1/3 cup)	white wine

PREPARATION OF HAZELNUT PRALINE

In a small, thick-bottom saucepan, thoroughly mix sugar and water. Bring to a boil, stirring constantly. Clean the sugar deposit forming around the saucepan using a small brush dipped in cold water. Stop stirring as soon as mixture begins to boil. Cook over moderate heat until mixture turns to a light caramel colour. Remove from heat. Add hazelnuts, immersing them in caramel. Pour onto a buttered baking sheet. Cool. Break the praline with a rolling pin, without crushing too much.

PROCEDURE

Cut assorted fruit into different shapes: cubes, quarters, wedges, slices.
Place egg yolks, sugar and white wine in a bain-marie. Over medium heat, whisk constantly until sabayon reaches a creamy but not frothy consistency.

FINAL PREPARATION AND PRESENTATION

Preheat oven broiler.
Place assorted fruit in dishes. Top with sabayon, and sprinkle with hazelnut praline. Grill for a few seconds on the oven's upper rack.

Blueberry Jam
and Scones

Makes 6 small jars

BLUEBERRY JAM

1.5 kg (3¹/₃ lb)	fresh blueberries
800 g (3¹/₂ cups)	granulated sugar
400 ml (1³/₄ cups)	maple syrup
45 ml (3 Tbsp)	fresh ginger, finely chopped

12 SCONES

200 g (1²/₃ cups)	flour
30 ml (2 Tbsp)	granulated sugar
15 ml (1 Tbsp)	baking powder
75 g (¹/₃ cup)	cold butter, cut into small cubes
125 ml (¹/₂ cup)	milk
1	egg, beaten

PREPARATION, 12 HOURS IN ADVANCE

Mix the ingredients for the jam and set aside at room temperature for 12 hours to allow sugar to dissolve.

PROCEDURE

The next day, bring mixture to a boil. Reduce heat and simmer for 10 minutes. Skim, if necessary, at the end of cooking. Pour jam into sterilized jars and close lids tightly. Identify the jars and cool.

PREPARATION OF THE SCONES

Preheat oven to 220°C (425°F). Mix together dry ingredients. Add cold butter and cut into dry ingredients until mixture becomes coarse. Add milk and mix.
Spread dough by hand to a thickness of about 2 cm (1 in). Cut with a round cookie cutter or slice into triangles. Place scones on a buttered cookie sheet, brush with a beaten egg and bake for 10 to 12 minutes, until golden.

PRESENTATION

Serve blueberry jam with hot scones for breakfast.

"I believe poetry is often revealed in the evening, at midnight on a day in July. I am staring at the expensive crystal-ware in the sky, and see bits and pieces of silver fall toward the lake; fireflies sizzle and dissolve."

Joe Rosenblatt

Iced Maple
Soufflé

Serves 6

200 ml (⁷/8 cup)	maple syrup
6	egg yolks
375 ml (1²/3 cups)	whipping cream

PROCEDURE, FIVE HOURS IN ADVANCE

In a saucepan, bring maple syrup to a boil. Reduce for 5 minutes to concentrate flavour.

In a bowl, beat egg yolks gently with a mixer. Then, beating constantly and vigorously, add maple syrup in a thin, steady stream. Continue to beat until mixture has cooled and thickened.

In a bowl, whip cream with a mixer until it forms peaks. Fold about one third of the whipped cream into the maple mixture. Carefully stir in the remaining cream.

Line the sides of small ramekins with a wax paper collar and pour in the mixture. Place in freezer for at least 4 hours.

FINAL PREPARATION AND PRESENTATION

In a small saucepan, reduce a few spoonfuls of maple syrup for a few minutes. Cool. Pour the cooled syrup onto the iced soufflés. Remove wax paper and serve immediately.

"...And turning over I embrace like a lover
the trunk of a tree, one of those
for whom the lightning was too much

and grew a brilliant
hunchback with a crown of leaves."

Irving Layton

Maple
Crème Brûlée

Serves 4

3	egg yolks
75 g (¹/₃ cup)	maple sugar
1	vanilla bean
50 ml (¹/₄ cup)	milk
300 ml (1¹/₃ cups)	whipping cream
60 ml (¹/₄ cup)	powdered maple sugar

PREPARATION, A FEW HOURS IN ADVANCE
In a bowl, beat egg yolks, sugar and vanilla bean cut lengthwise and scraped. Add milk and stir well. Add whipping cream and continue stirring. Allow mixture to infuse for 10 minutes.

Preheat oven to 150°C (300°F).

Pass mixture through a fine sieve and pour into ramekins. Place in a shallow baking pan filled with boiling water to half the height of the ramekins. Bake for about 45 minutes, or until cream remains firm when the ramekins are moved. Chill a few hours.

FINAL PREPARATION AND PRESENTATION
Sprinkle each ramekin with powdered maple sugar. Caramelize under the oven broiler. Serve crème brûlée warm or chilled.

Chocolate Volcano
à la Véronique

Serves 12

GANACHE

265 ml (1¼ cups)	whipping cream
20 ml (4 tsp)	maple syrup
10 ml (2 tsp)	Grand Marnier ®
	or other orange liqueur
7 ml (1½ tsp)	vanilla extract
½	orange zest
165 g (6 oz)	milk chocolate chunks

CARAMELIZED SUGAR

200 g (1 cup)	granulated sugar
	water to moisten
225 ml (1 cup)	strong, hot coffee
175 g (6 oz)	bitter chocolate
250 g (1⅛ cups)	unsalted butter
200 g (1 cup)	granulated sugar
6	eggs
200 g (1½ cups)	flour
1 g (¼ tsp)	salt
2 g (½ tsp)	baking powder

**PREPARATION OF GANACHE,
12 HOURS IN ADVANCE**

Bring to a boil the cream, maple syrup, orange liqueur, vanilla extract and orange zest. Pour hot mixture onto milk chocolate chunks. Stir gently until smooth and chocolate is melted.

Cover a 12-mould ice cube tray with plastic wrap. Pour in mixture and freeze for 12 hours.

PROCEDURE

Preheat oven to 180°C (350°F).

Pour hot coffee onto bitter chocolate pieces, stir gently until smooth and chocolate is melted.

Cream butter and sugar. Beating constantly, add eggs, one at a time.

Without stirring too much, alternately add remaining dry ingredients and coffee preparation until almost smooth. In 12 individual buttered and floured cupcake moulds, pour in a bit of the cake preparation and top each with a frozen ganache. Pour remaining cake batter to cover. Bake for 25 to 30 minutes.

PREPARATION OF CARAMELIZED SUGAR

Moisten sugar with water. Bring to a boil and cook to 142°C (287°F). Pour immediately in a thin, steady stream on parchment paper to create interesting patterns.

PRESENTATION

Place hot volcano on dessert plate and cover with partially whipped cream. Garnish with caramelized sugar.

Recipe by Véronique Gosselin

An enchanted country...

Icewine
Chocolates

Makes 2 dozen

120 g (4 oz)   **molding chocolate**

ICEWINE GANACHE
75 ml (¹/3 cup)   **whipping cream**
25 ml (2 Tbsp)   **glucose *or* corn syrup**
200 g (7 oz)   **dark chocolate**
40 g (3 Tbsp)   **unsalted butter**
150 ml (²/3 cup)   **icewine**

PROCEDURE, A FEW HOURS IN ADVANCE
In a bain-marie, melt chocolate to a maximum of 52°C (125°F). Remove from bain-marie and stir constantly to bring temperature down to 28°C (82°F). Return to bain-marie and raise temperature to 33°C (92°F). This is called tempering chocolate.
With a brush, thinly coat clean moulds with tempered chocolate. Allow to harden.
Pour melted chocolate into moulds, filling them; tap on moulds to remove air bubbles. Place moulds over tempered chocolate, let drip and harden for a few hours.

PREPARATION OF ICEWINE GANACHE
In a saucepan, mix cream and glucose or corn syrup. Bring to a boil.

Chop chocolate. Pour hot mixture over chocolate and whisk briskly. Cool, add butter and icewine. Whisk until ganache is smooth.
If necessary, gently reheat ganache in a bain-marie to liquefy slightly. Using a pastry bag, fill cavities of chocolate moulds with ganache, leaving a little space for chocolate bottom. Allow to dry in a cool place for a few hours.
Melt chocolate as you did before. Complete filling moulds with tempered chocolate. Set aside and cool.

PRESENTATION
Remove from moulds and serve chocolates with a glass of chilled icewine...

Recipe index

"In nature, a kind of art is at work, a type of oriented
        technical capacity that works the substance from within.
The form seizes the matter, and suppresses indetermination."

Aristotle

Who can say it better?
Hubert Reeves